Wee Boys from Glasgow Don't Cry

Peter Stanway

Cover design by Peter Stanway
WEE BOYS FROM GLASGOW DON'T CRY
© 2010 by Peter Stanway
Published by RevMedia Publishing

ISBN 978-09772194-4-5

Library of Congress Control Number: 2010939685

Printed in the United States of America and United Kingdom

For Information:
RevMedia Publishing
Po Box 5172
Kingwood, TX 77325
USA
www.revmediapublishing.com
www.revministries.com
www.revmedianetwork.com
www.revmediatv.com

To contact Peter Stanway: www.peterstanwaybooks.com
See back page for more details.

NAMES DISCLAIMER

Many of the names of the characters in this book have been changed to protect their identity.

DEDICATION

For all the people who have helped me when I couldn't help
myself,
especially for my amazing wife Nancy.
Thank you.

TABLE OF CONTENTS

FOREWORD

Anybody who knows Peter Stanway will find this book a fascinating read. He is truly a trophy of God's grace, saved from a life that on several occasions could have ended prematurely in disaster, and saved for a ministry that would impact the lives of many with the reality of God's love.

Peter spares us unnecessary details and keeps the narrative moving at break-neck speed – much like his early life, but in a very different way! So your interest will not flag as you are taken from one unlikely scenario to another.

Reading this book demonstrated for me that great truth that when God decides to place His hand on someone's life, He will ensure that His purpose in doing so will be fulfilled. It is amazing what He will allow someone to go through before plucking them out of the mire and placing them in Christ Jesus. A life that was full of darkness becomes a shining light that can carry the truth to others.

I trust that many who have no hope will read the book, those who feel that they have messed up their lives completely, whether through their own failings or by being the victim of circumstances. This book will surely give them hope and encouragement, for no problem is too great for Jesus Christ to deal with. He gave His life for the hopeless, those who have no self-worth. He alone can make them new.

Those who have known the Lord personally for many years will find this an encouraging read, demonstrating that there is always more to reach out to receive from our Lord, more that He wants to impart to us and more that He wants to do with us for His glory.

All who read this book will surely join with Peter in saying: "Thank you, Lord, for your love, your mercy and your grace!"

Colin Urquhart
Apostle and Founder of Kingdom Faith Ministries
www.kingdomfaith.com

INTRODUCTION

Whenever I shared stories from my life with others, they would invariably say, 'You should write a book'. Well, here it is!

In writing, *Wee boys from Glasgow Don't Cry*, my aim is to encourage every reader not to give up. No matter what the circumstances there is always hope, no matter how many times we mess up, there is always hope.

My desire is that this message of hope will reach as many people as possible regardless of background, colour or culture. This is not a religious book, rather it is a book for people who long for an awesome personal relationship with someone who will love them unconditionally.

There is nothing superficial within these pages. Every word is here for a reason. Everything that happened to me, happened for a reason. Looking back, I can see how the pieces of my life fit together and make sense – even the bad stuff.

God worked through people and permitted circumstances to bring me to Himself. I still had a choice. With nothing to lose, I made the right one......

"Wee Boys from Glasgow Don't Cry is a challenging real-life roller-coaster story of survival and victory. In the twilight zone of drugs and alcohol, Peter spirals deeper into a desperate lifestyle with no holds barred. On the run with another man's wife, extreme personal transformation is just about to hit him! Completely dysfunctional from years of hedonism he is thrown a lifeline from where he last expected. With no options left, Peter grabs the outstretched hand of Jesus. The power of God knocks him to the floor. When he gets up he is totally changed. The real adventure is about to begin ....."

1

WEE BOYS FROM GLASGOW DON'T CRY

The sickening, all-too-familiar sound of exploding rage interrupted my sleep. Although I could not see what was happening, my mind added graphic images to the sounds I heard. As my mother lay helpless on the floor outside my bedroom, kicks and punches were viciously pummeled into her body. The stoic brokenness of her sobs went pathetically unheard amidst the demonic, drunken, roar of my dad's death threats. In a frenzy of jealousy he screamed accusations loud enough to be heard over the sound of water gushing into the bath in which he was going to drown her…... Frustrated, angry, and hurting, I choked back my tears because wee boys from Glasgow don't cry. With all the strength a five-year-old could muster, I beat-up my pillow, wishing it was my dad. Finally, exhausted, I fell back into a fitful sleep.

In the morning, I nervously surveyed the scene from the night before. Mum's sodden black beehive hairpiece lay limp on the floor like a dead, drowned cat. For the next few days my mum took to bed, unable to walk properly and too ashamed to show her cuts and bruises to the neighbors. As if they didn't know. Eventually with dark sunglasses donned, life began to revert back to something like normal, for a little while.

I was born on June 24th 1956, weighing in at around ten pounds. I was born by caesarean section; the first-born child of Barbara and Alex Stanway, at the Rottenrow Hospital, Glasgow. My mum was eighteen years old and my dad was twenty-one. For a few months after I was born we lived in London Road, Bridgeton in Glasgow's East End. After that, we moved to a top floor flat in a tenement building in Hamilton Road, Rutherglen, three miles southwest of Glasgow City Centre.

One of my earliest memories is of sitting mesmerized but safe on my Uncle Danny's shoulders. We watched three fire engines and countless firemen trying to bring the blaze under control as the whole top landing, top floor, went up in flames. I almost died in that fire at the tender age of four years. The sound of terror in the middle of the night woke me up; the smoke was too thick to see through. I made my way into the bedroom wardrobe, presumably thinking I would be safe there. The door clicked closed behind me, in effect, saving me from being overcome by smoke or burned by the flames licking their way around the wardrobe.

In a panic, everyone had left the building. When my dad realized I was missing, he raced back up the stairs and into my bedroom, but he couldn't see me. By the grace of God he heard me in the wardrobe, ripped off the door and rescued me. We made the front page of the evening newspaper, the *Evening Citizen*. I was unscathed but my dad suffered burns and sported a few heroes' bandages.

The *Evening Citizen* article from May 13th, 1961 read, headline: 'Fire Rescue Drama', sub-heading: 'Father saves son – then collapses'. It then went on to say;
'A young father, with his son in his arms, was found unconscious in the smoke-filled stairway of a Rutherglen tenement early today as flames swept through his three-bedroom flat Twenty-five-year old Mr Alex Stanway snatched his four-year-old boy from his bedroom and then dashed through a wall of fire. He was badly burned on the head and arms and collapsed when he reached the stair – still clutching young Peter. The fire started in the kitchen. The family had struggled through flames and smoke to the stairhead when Mr Stanway realised that Peter was missing. He ignored the neighbour's pleas to wait for the firemen and dashed back into his burning home – despite the intense heat.

He staggered back out with Peter and collapsed.

Said Mr Stanway: 'I just remember running back but everything else is blank. I don't even remember getting Peter out of his room.'

Said his pretty wife Barbara: 'I don't know how Alex did it. We couldn't even breathe in the stairway. I was thankful to see them both safe.'

A neighbour said: 'Alex was still cuddling his little boy in his arms despite his injuries. The flames were leaping through the roof – the heat was so fierce that it melted my daughter's wedding picture off the wall'.

2

GROWING UP – PRIMARY SCHOOL

My gran and grandpa also lived in Rutherglen. Since the fire destroyed our flat in Hamilton Road, we all moved in with them. They loved me. Almost every Saturday evening my grandpa would take me by the hand and walk me up to Carolla's Café for an ice cream. Afterwards, we listened to the Salvation Army Band who gathered in a circle on Rutherglen's wide Main Street with brass instruments and tambourines, singing and, no doubt, sharing messages about Jesus.

Within a year of the fire we were re-housed to a brand new maisonette in Fernhill, near Rutherglen. Since Fernhill was still being built, for a young child, it was like moving into a giant adventure playground. I had windows to jump out of onto mountains of sand, and dens to build from fencing posts. Not only that we were on the edge of the countryside with Cathkin Braes behind us and the 'Rocky' and 'Bluebell' woods beside us.

The 'Rockies' had a rock-face with huge tree roots strewn across it, behind which, I believed, was a secret Aladdin's cave filled with uncountable treasure. Most days in the summer I would chip away with tools of my own invention, totally convinced that one day I would break through and discover that hidden store of shimmering treasure.

The 'Bluebells' were a carpet of bluebell flowers in springtime and a magnificent skating pond in winter. I remember camping there, feeling petrified, one summer evening. The bigger boys told us ghost stories as one of them sneaked out of the tent without us seeing him. He picked up a broken branch from a tree and began scratching on the outside of the tent. Well, I scampered like a greyhound from a trap and headed for home. My haste was hampered when I stepped on a piece of wood with a nail in it left behind by some workmen. "A foot in my nail! A foot in my nail!" I hollered traumatised and confused as I crashed through the door and reached the sanctuary of my house.

On another occasion I fell down into the foundations to what would become "the shops". Unfortunately, I landed onto a discarded milk bottle which broke under the impact. Blood spurted everywhere! I had sustained a nasty gash on my leg and a man who was passing-by helped me home. It was decided that I needed stitches in the wound. Since we didn't have a car, the next door neighbour 'Old Pat' was recruited to drive me to the hospital in his electric milk float, at a speed of ten to fifteen miles per hour. We eventually got there before I bled to death and my leg was stitched up.

By now, the mid 1960's, I had a brother and sister. 'Wee Alex', who was born between my sister and me, had died from 'cot death syndrome' as a baby so there was six years between myself and Barbara; seven between myself and Stephen. My primary school, Cathkin Primary School, where my education began, was about half an hour's walk away.

I remember one of my teachers, Mrs Litton, who was quite eccentric. She said that it was all right for us to eat sweets in class, so long as we brought in enough to share with everyone. Every Friday she would bring in a huge bag of sweets and gave them out to the whole class. However, if any of us ever misbehaved at any time, she would drag the offenders to the front of the class to make an example of them. She would shout at him or her while pushing and shaking them about by the arm. I even remember her, on occasion, she stood on top of her desk to emphasise some point that she was making. Even although she was 'scary' I can still remember many of the lessons that she taught us.

There was no regular or dependable bus service up to Fernhill so most of the people living there had to walk up the big hill (Fern*hill*) from Rutherglen. Often young mothers with young families could be seen pushing a heavy Silver Cross pram laden with babies and their weekly shopping. Part of this journey meant passing 'the hole in the wall', (which was precisely that – a hole in the wall that separated Castlemilk from Fernhill), that led into Castlemilk (a huge housing 'scheme', i.e. the Glasgow word for housing development). From time-to-time, characters like Wellington Willie or Sandshoe Sannie would jump out from behind the wall and stretch wide their raincoats to reveal that all they were wearing was the footwear that gave them their names.

Friday night, pay day for the workers, usually meant that the last bus up the hill (the number 21), if it was running, was overfilled with passengers who had enjoyed the hospitality of the pubs in Rutherglen that had, in turn, enjoyed taking their well-earned wages off them. As the bus struggled up the hill I remember on one occasion steam coming out from the engine and someone shouting out, 'It's well seen it's a Friday, even the bus is steaming!'

I was bigger than most of the boys my age and, as such, if you were after a reputation, I was the one to beat in a fight. It wasn't that I was a good fighter - I hated fighting, but the glory hunters picked fights with me and after a while, I learned to stand-up for myself. Unfortunately, this fighting continued outside the school playground and I remember my dad hanging out of the living room window throwing coins down onto the concrete slabs below as he placed bets on me winning fights with challengers who were twice my size. Although I fought as hard as I could to save myself and please my dad, I invariably lost which meant that my dad also lost his money and that led to him finishing-off what the bullies had started when I got up the stairs. It was a lose-lose situation.

Once, I tried to act tough with a girl who was a bit of a tomboy. We both zoomed down our steep pavement each sitting on a big hard-backed book that was balanced on top of an old metal roller-skate (the forerunner of the skateboard). I knocked her off on the way down and she waited for me to walk back up to where I had 'ditched her'. She whacked me across the head with her skate, leaving a scar just above my left eye, which is still there to this day as a constant reminder to never underestimate the fairer sex!

I also remember some great times growing up in Fernhill – like the long summer holidays from school when a small group of us would walk up past Cathkin Braes to the reservoir beyond to go swimming. In winter, it was sledging-time down the big hill that led to 'The Varneys' - the posh houses at the bottom of the hill. We steered the sledge with our feet lying on our stomachs until our wellies (Wellington boots) were so full of snow that our feet went numb. I remember the pain of thawing out my feet in front of the electric fire back home and then the immense relief when I could feel my toes again.

3

GROWING UP – SECONDARY SCHOOL

At twelve years old, I went to Rutherglen Academy which was about an hour away from our home in Fernhill but only ten minutes from where my grandparents lived. It being so close, I often stayed there with them.

After two years the whole school was moved into a new comprehensive, Cathkin High, and for a time I started staying at home more often. However, things were difficult at home. Mum and dad argued more and more frequently and violently. My mum required pills and regular hospitalisation.

I joined the Boy's Brigade, which meant that I was out most nights. I played rugby for the school and began jogging in the evenings. My dad thought it was 'sissy' to play rugby and not football, so he decided to 'make a man of me' by encouraging me to fight. Whenever I lost, I wept bitterly both at losing the contest and losing face with my dad. I wanted 'to be a man' but those defeats made me a sissy in his eyes. I began to hate him. To get away I would jog about one-hundred miles a week, plus any other training I could do with the school or the Boy's Brigade. I started to run cross-country marathons. I was fit but lonely.

During those years I met my first love, it was the first time I had ever felt those kind of butterflies inside. Although the romance didn't last very long, I will never forget those feelings. I don't even remember kissing, just those exciting, goose-bumpy feelings all over. Trisha was a lovely girl but she was a Roman Catholic. My dad hated Catholics so there was never any hope for a future in that relationship.

Around the age of fourteen I met a friend at school who was the son of a minister at the church where the Boy's Brigade met. George wasn't interested in the Boy's Brigade; he preferred drugs instead. We started hitch-hiking at the weekends, and although drugs and alcohol were around, I wasn't very interested. We would sleep rough in fields and bus shelters and I loved it!

I had found freedom and adventure. Soon I was hitch hiking further and further a field, with or without George. I remember once being on my own and stranded late at night on the old A66 between Scotch Corner and Penrith. I saw a light in the distance and made my way towards what turned out to be an isolated farmhouse. I asked the farmer if I could take shelter in his barn for the night and he chased me off his land.

Dejected but excited I made my way back to the dark, and now quiet, road. I found a long, straight stretch where the car's headlights would pick me out from a distance and could pull in and stop. Eventually a car did stop. There were four hippies inside and they were all laughing and having a good time. They offered me some cannabis to smoke and it made me feel strange but good. As it turned out, one of the girls had attended a convent school in Fernhill! She was returning there to visit so they dropped me off right outside my house. The next day I tried to make sense of what had happened and, by and large, I felt good about it, especially the effects of the cannabis.....

When I was about fifteen years old I began seeking new depths and heights of escapism. I began to discover outlets through my mind. Existentialism, transcendental meditation, philosophy and, at the same time, drugs and alcohol became features in my life. In pursuit of fulfilment, fantasy crept in.

About this time a Christian geography teacher at school had taken an interest in a group of us. With our parent's consent, he and his wife had invited us to their home for a curry meal. I was impressed that they had taken a long time to prepare it and had gone to great lengths to make our experience enjoyable. Their friendship and hospitality made it a relaxed evening and in that atmosphere they presented the Christian gospel to us. I went home, gave it a lot of thought and concluded that I wanted to become a Christian. In my grandparent's home, in my bedroom, I went down on my knees and I asked Jesus into my heart. I sincerely wanted to be a Christian. I meant it!

I started to attend Christian meetings and went to the Christian Union in our school and other schools. I did this for a few months but, tragically, I knew nothing about the Holy Spirit. The Holy Spirit gives Christians strength and power to follow Jesus. I had a two-cylinder faith, Father and Son but no Holy Spirit, the source of strength and power to follow Jesus. Therefore, in my own strength, it was too difficult to continue being a Christian. At that time, if I had told my dad that I had been baptized in the Holy Spirit, he would have taken that to mean I had become a Catholic and that would have resulted in him giving me a severe beating.

A few months later I began to backslide deeper into sin-filled fantasy through books, music, drugs, alcohol and sex ....

4

HITCHING ON THE HIGHWAYS

On my sixteenth birthday I began hitchhiking through Europe. I remember on the morning of my sixteenth birthday (the legal age to apply for a passport without parental consent), I was in the port of Dover waiting outside the main post office for it to open. I had brought all the necessary documents and was issued with a one-year 'British Visitors passport' (no longer available). By late afternoon that day I was hitchhiking my way to Paris.

Although I had hitched around Britain for a couple of years, I was still young and quite naive. My main lift into Paris turned out to be from some Italian anarchists who were on their way to blow up something there! I managed to get dropped off before their destination and found myself wandering alone in this large foreign city as evening progressed into night.

I sat on the steps of the *Sacré-Coeur* Basilica with the other hippies and listened as they sang and played guitar. After a while I went for a walk around Montmartre and watched the artists. When I returned to the steps everyone had gone. I had a cheap sleeping bag (costing me 50 pence in a fire sale), but it was too steep to sleep on the embankments. I walked to the bottom of the steps and made my way along a dimly lit path covered with overhanging trees following the course of the river Seine.

Up ahead I saw a small group of shadowy figures gathered together under the muted light of a dim street lamp. As I passed them, I noticed they were black-skinned. One of them reached out to turn me by the shoulder. 'Sorry friend, he said in deeply accented French, 'but times are hard'. Due to my poor French and his accent, it seemed to take ages before it dawned on me what he meant. I understood just as his other arm went up and in his hand he held a huge machete.

I took to my heels and bolted back towards the stairs, taking them two or three at a time as he chased after me. I felt a thud on the back of my head but kept on running. After what seemed ages, I found myself alone in a quiet neighborhood where the apartments had a door onto the pavement and another door inside leading to the houses. I settled between the two doors. Once I had caught my breath and my heart had slowed down to the speed of a runaway train, I removed my backpack, which was designed with a high back. On examination, I discovered a hole through the pack into the contents inside, right where my head would have been. That high pack had stopped the machete from hitting the back of my head and had saved my life.

Undeterred by this experience, I went on many more European adventures over the next few years. Once, a well meaning Dutch couple on holiday drove hundreds of miles out of their way to take me to the Susten Pass, high up in the Swiss Alps. They did this in order for me to hitch another lift down the other side into Italy. However, as the day wore on, the traffic grew less and less until there was none. I was stranded at over six thousand feet up in the mountains with snow all around. You could spit peas through my 50p sleeping bag. I had no winter clothes. I had visions of dying of exposure (you can die of exposure in Scotland at a height of three thousand feet or less!). Desperate for shelter, I tried the door of a small café, now closed for business. It was still unlocked and a girl gave me some whiskey and a blanket. Needless to say, I survived despite the odds.

The next day I began walking towards Italy. Very unusually, a biker riding a huge chopper stopped, pulled his bike off the road and offered to smoke some hash laced with opium with me.

He left me a chunk and went on his way. Darkness began to fall and it stated to rain. I found a small cave in which to shelter. As the weather worsened, I watched the most amazing cosmic display of God's power that I have ever seen. Perhaps it was enhanced with drugs I had taken but I sat amazed as forked lightening exploded off the surrounding mountains illuminating the black sky and thunder boomed and rumbled as though it was the end of the world. After hours, the storm abated and the sky lightened and I resumed hitch hiking. A couple stopped for me and dropped me off in Como, a breathtaking picturesque Alpine Italian village, edged by the lake of the same name.

My sojourns were to take me repeatedly through Italy, France, Germany Switzerland, Belgium and Holland. I was such a frequent visitor to France that I began speaking French fluently. Most of the time I enjoyed the freedom of hitch-hiking on my own; I learned how to do it quite successfully. I could virtually pick the car I wanted and make it stop. In the early days I would go where the cars were going. Later I could decide where I was going and hitch-hike my way there. As time went on I travelled with less and less baggage – usually just my trusty 50p sleeping bag and a couple of essentials rolled-up inside. I ate very little, usually surviving on bread and milk or yoghurt.

I also often went to Amsterdam because I enjoyed the art galleries and the people there. One sunny day in the early 1970s, I sat with lots of other people in Vondelpark in the town centre. A long-haired policeman came up to a group of us who were smoking cannabis. Looking straight at me, he took the joint from me and, sniffing the smoke, he asked me if it was cannabis. He took a couple of deep inhalations and handing it back to me he said, 'yes, it is' and went on his way. I thought I was going to be bust. I hadn't realised that smoking hash was accepted in designated areas in Amsterdam. The Paradiso was a night club in downtown

Amsterdam where live bands played and sold drugs were sold legally. I was freaked-out and blown away by such liberality.

These wanderings occurred mostly during my school holidays, as I hadn't yet finished school. While I was at home, now living permanently with my grandparents, I drank more and took drugs regularly. I now stayed permanently with my grandparents. I grew my hair long, took LSD and got into rock music. A group of us often played truant together and went off to the local park with some bottles of wine and some 'recreational' drugs.

About this time, I met a girl called Carol and our relationship began to deepen. I was ready to leave school at the age of sixteen, but Carol, who had decided to stay on, talked me into doing the same. She suggested that I try to get the qualifications and the portfolio necessary to go to Art School in Glasgow. It sounded like a good idea.

5

ART SCHOOL

'You need a haircut! And in your case its feet not inches!' the deputy headmaster hollered at me. I also needed to restart the subjects I had dropped, including art, and to try to build up a good portfolio of practical work by attending art school in the evenings.

Amazingly, I passed all my Higher exams (now called A Levels or GCSEs), compiled a good enough portfolio and was accepted for the Glasgow School of Art in the autumn of 1974. I could hardly believe it. The Glasgow School of Art had a worldwide reputation largely due to its Charles Rennie Mackintosh connections. I had expectations of joining a community where genius and frenzied creative activity made it unique. I was to be disappointed ....

To help me get around, I decided to buy myself some 'wheels' with a part of the grant money I had been awarded as a full-time student; a little red Vespa 90cc scooter. The scooter was dirt cheap. The night I drove it home from a garage in the city centre, it was pouring down with rain and it was the middle of the rush hour. I had no idea about gears, so I drove it all the way home in first gear. Knowing nothing about the Highway Code, it's a miracle I made it home at all!

My favourite memories were driving to my 'secret place' on the River Avon near Strathaven about on hour from Rutherglen. This was a place that was to become significant at different times throughout my life, as you will learn later.
I was a terrible driver and didn't really get any better as time went on. I would attempt hill starts, and the scooter would shoot ahead and leave me standing. Once I was knocked off when turning right into my grandparents' house, and that scared me.

I only had the scooter for a few months before my dad bought it from me, but I don't think that he was any better a driver than I was. He kept it only a few months before he sold it. We were both glad to see the back of it.

During my first year as a student (on Carol's birthday, February 19th) my mum made another suicide attempt. She had been with Carol and me and, having drunk too much, went home and took handfuls of strong prescription drugs. A few hours later, in a very slurred voice she called me up to say 'goodbye'. When I reached her house, my dad, who had been at the pub, was in a deep, drunken sleep. I poured black coffee into my mum and walked her up and down the living room floor until the ambulance arrived. I went with her to the hospital where she had her stomach pumped and was then admitted to the psychiatric ward.

At daybreak when I returned to her home just as dad began to waken up...
'Where's your mother?'My dad asked with his tongue sticking to his parched throat.
'She's in hospital after a suicide attempt.' I answered. He shrugged his shoulders uncaringly. We had all been through this many times before.
'This time it's serious dad, she almost died.' He wasn't quite grasping what I said as he stared blankly at the floor.
'It's time for you both to stop drinking alcohol.' I stated and over the next week to ten days I never let my dad out of my sight. I found out where Alcoholics Anonymous meetings were held and I dragged him there, morning noon and night - all over Glasgow and all over Central Scotland. From that day on he never drank alcohol again and neither did my mother.

To my great disappointment I discovered that, with one or two exceptions, most of the first year foundations students didn't really want to be at Art School. I learned that they were there because of the prestige for their families or because they didn't have the brains to go to university.

For my part, I naively thought that I wanted to be a fine artist majoring on drawing and painting. I began to realize that art was far more encompassing than that. I was attracted to multi-media and performance art and to the work of the Abstract Expressionists like Pollock, De Kooning and Franz Kline among others.

I continued my trips abroad, which now including essential visits to famous art galleries. I drooled in front of masterpieces old and modern in The Louvre and in the Gallery of the French Impressionists in Paris; also in the Rembrandt Museum, the Van Gogh Museum and the Museum of Modern Art in Amsterdam, not forgetting our own rich heritage in Scotland and the UK.

My Bohemian lifestyle and hedonistic extremism led me into many tangents of worthless frivolity yet, despite all that, I asked Carol to marry me. At the end of the second year, a handful of us at the Art School created a new department called 'Mixed Media' where we were free to experiment with new mediums like video and performance art and incorporate it with modern expressions of fine art. At the end of this year, I was well and truly spaced out! I decided to leave art school after completing three years and marry Carol.

Much to my surprise the head of the Painting Department offered me the use of his villa in the south of France where I could have a few months to think it over. Apparently, I was doing better with my tutor's assessments than I thought, but my mind was made up; I was leaving ('on sabbatical').

In April 1977 I married Carol. We lived in a rented tenement flat in Rutherglen. I worked in a bedding factory - the same one in which

I had worked during some of the holidays from Art School. Carol's dad was a manager there and her mum a machinist. Before too long I became works manager with the responsibility for fifty people. I knew, however, that this was not what I was meant to do with my life and I wasn't being fulfilled. After two years I left and, to 'clear my head', I worked on a building site for a few months.

To get that job, I walked for many miles from one end of Glasgow to the other visiting every building site I passed. On my way I met a man who had experience of working on the sites, however, he couldn't read or write. We agreed, therefore, that I would fill in our application forms and write what he told me to say. On our forms we were 'compressor men'. It all sounded very impressive and we were offered jobs.

I had no idea what I was letting myself in for! On the first morning we were given jackhammers and put down a twelve-foot. Supporting the jackhammer on my chest, I had to drill horizontally into the rocks in front of me.

At the end of a week I was aching in places I didn't know I had. I couldn't wash because there was no part of my hands where the skin was not open and, apart from that, they were locked permanently in the 'grip' position. It didn't take long to come to my senses and realize this was not for me.

Around this time, I spent some time out and about in the streets of Rutherglen snapping pictures of interesting people and events. Some of these I sold to individuals and others I sold to local and national newspapers ('the singing bus driver'/'the one hundred year old dog'). I registered with the BFP (The Bureau of Freelance Photographers) and started to lodge photos with London-based agencies. I still drew and painted a little and received some good commissions.

Occasionally, I worked with children's groups on creative projects and taught art to aspiring artists.

Carol became pregnant with our first child and our beautiful daughter, Sarah, was born in April 1980. Coinciding almost exactly with her birth, I opened my first studio/gallery in Hamilton Road, Rutherglen, not far from where I had almost died in the tenement fire at the age of four.

6

"SCOTLAND'S TOP ROCK AND POP PHOTOGRAPHER"

Initially, I took all sorts of photographs: weddings, babies, even pets! This branched out to include commercial, industrial, even criminal injuries, but eventually a large portion of my work was for the national press.

Due to my love for music, my work soon evolved into shooting for the music tabloids and record companies. As this progressed I often worked two or three concerts in one evening – rushing back to develop the photos (these were the pre-digital days!) and to express parcel them to the London offices of the music tabloids overnight. If I had commitments to shoot in the daytime, I would have to fulfill them before going out to cover more bands in the evening.

As demand for my work grew, I started travelling to London on a regular basis. Eventually this meant being in London every week, usually travelling overnight to give me a working day both ends. My consumption of alcohol and drugs rose to terrifying quantities during this time; especially my consumption of amphetamines, mainly speed and sometimes cocaine. When I had a chance to sleep, I would take 'downers' leading eventually to heroin. This 'balancing act' was unsustainable and both my body and mind became seriously affected. My marriage was also falling apart as I hardly ever saw Carol and Sarah.

At the same time my professional reputation was growing and I started to receive front page jobs. Spandau Ballet for *Record Mirror* was the first. I worked with famous people and covered major music events. In total I worked with over five hundred different bands. At a Punk Festival in Leeds that I covered, I stood in front of the stage in the photographers' pit between the bands and the crowd. After the festival, as a result of the deluge of spitting and both the fans and bands throwing alcohol at each other, I had to burn the clothes I had been wearing.

The Arts Council asked me to exhibit in their UK galleries and hailed me as 'Scotland's Top Rock and Pop Photographer'. My earnings rose (sometimes up to one thousand pounds a day) and so did my expenses (sometimes more than one thousand pounds per day!). As Carol and I became more distant, I began a new relationship with a journalist, Olivia. Dazed and confused by drugs, alcohol, and my crazy lifestyle, I was unfaithful to Carol. She left me and I went into a tailspin.

My lifestyle was a 'Frankenstein', a monster that would kill me. Looking for a way out, I stopped taking future commissions and tried to work more locally. Initially this went well but I soon became bored. It began to dawn on me that the size of my drugs and alcohol habit was big enough to kill an elephant and I also missed the adrenalin rush from the concert work.

My next step was to use the many influential contacts I had made through the music industry to begin a promotion business. Soon I was promoting live bands and music events throughout Central Scotland and operated in five night clubs simultaneously. Enter 'Frankenstein Mark II' . . .

I started managing up-and-coming bands, the most successful of which was a Christian band called 'Woza', later to morph into 'Deacon Blue'. I knew a little about Christianity, enough to 'talk the talk' when arranging gigs (concerts) for the band. Around this time while doing a Radio Clyde radio interview with them, DJ Billy Sloan, who had written the Spandau Ballet feature for which

I had taken the photos, ironically talked of the 'messianic zeal' of Peter Stanway.

The band graciously left me to my pagan ways. Although, in retrospect, God had begun a process of turning my life around and bringing me back to Himself. I had been in and out of hospitals and on prescribed medication from various doctors, but now I was determined that if I was going to save my marriage and my life, I needed to take some drastic action. The year was 1983, and I was about to enter a rehabilitation centre for the first time.

7

RUNNING AWAY

I went to a near derelict ex-Catholic seminary in Cardross between Helensburgh and Dumbarton, run by a man called Willie Blainey. I stayed for a volatile nine months. Not everyone who came was serious about kicking their habit. Some came to review their habit and their expenses, and left after a short time to start all over again with a more affordable habit. Some came determined to change and lasted from days to months before falling. Others came looking for leniency at pending court appearances. In my own case, I did well for the first few weeks. I came through cold turkey and all withdrawals. My body was doing fine but my head was still messed-up.

One night there was an immensely powerful electric storm that had an effect on the adrenalin of some of the younger boys. One of them decided that he would go outside and play tag with the lightning bolts, dodging them as they exploded around the grounds of the house. When he came back in his hair was standing vertically and his eyes were like organ-stops. He was high with the rush of his near death experience and, in a way, it is that same tag-match with death that drives some people to become addicts. Another boy came in via hospital where he had almost died from taking heroin that had been cut with Vim cleaning powder. This concoction had burned away parts of his vital organs almost destroying his heart. After a couple of weeks of rehabilitation he left and went straight back to the same pusher he had bought that stuff from.

When I received a clothing grant from the DHS, another addict and I went straight to a dealer's house, bought heroin and a set of works (a needle and syringe), went into a city centre bar and shot up. I was second on the needle so I flushed the works out in the toilet cistern. When we returned to the rehab, it was clear from our actions and our eyes that we had taken drugs. However, they gave us another chance. Three days later my skin turned the color of a banana and my eyes blood red like Dracula. I had caught the Hepatitis virus. The doctor told me it was classified as 'Non A – Non B' and that there would be no lasting side effects. Therefore, when I recovered I never thought about it again (for almost twenty years).

After six months more in rehab, Carol began to visit me. It looked possible that there could be reconciliation between us. I began to apply for jobs and I was accepted as a co-ordinator with a large 'gingerbread' group, a single parent organisation, based in Dennistoun in the east end of Glasgow. It went well for a few months. I remained clean and sober. I was reunited with my wife and daughter and stayed with them. Carol became pregnant again with our son, Ryan.

At the worst possible time, while in the throes of helping to organise a huge national youth event, I fell back on my old ways, got drunk, disgraced myself and my family and pushed my marriage beyond redemption. At that point of no return, I decided enough was enough and made up my mind to run away, disappearing into the sunset. I resolved to head for Africa and whether I ended up on the east or west coast would determine the direction I would take after that. I threw myself into my own farewell party, which lasted for several days.

I had arranged to connect with a trans-European truck driver who would take me to Spain. By the time I finally got myself together enough to leave, I had no money, no wife and virtually no hope. I was borderline insane at this time, in the early stages of a nervous breakdown and rapidly losing any kind of hold on reality.

Leap-frogging trucks across Europe I eventually stopped off in Cordoba in Andalusia in Southern Spain. It was September/October 1986. I didn't speak Spanish at that time, but I did speak French. I located a French-speaking taxi driver and he took me to a Spanish/French speaking owner of a small hotel. After a couple of days I located the best language school in the city. I showed them my forged TEFL (Teaching English as a Foreign Language) certificate and was employed there as a conversation teacher.

My students were all fluent in English and only needed conversation practice. In the course of doing this, I began to learn Spanish from my students. I soon began to become the worse for drinking huge amounts of wine. I became sick and couldn't hold down the job. They discovered that I had forged the qualification and sacked me. Plans to charge me were later dropped. While I was a teacher, I had made good friends among my students, many of whom were mature businessmen. They asked if I would continue to teach them privately.

One of my students had a girlfriend, who had a friend … her name was Inmaculada de le Concepcion, or Inma for short. She became my girlfriend … I grew to deeply love Inma, her children and her family. Her parents, who were separated, sold lottery tickets for ONCE - Organización Nacional de Ciegos de España (The National Organization of Blind People in Spain) a Spanish organisation that helps the blind and partially sighted. Her mother had one eye and her father was completely blind. Aida and Sylvia, Inma's daughters, had different fathers. Inma worked cleaning houses and lived with and looked after her dad.

Not long after we met, we rented an apartment in La Juderia, the fascinating old Jewish neighbourhood in the beautiful city of Cordoba, not far from La Mezquita, which was, when it was built in the eighth century, the second largest mosque in the world after Mecca. It was from our apartment or in my student's homes that I taught English as a foreign language until, like a repeating nightmare, alcohol again took its toll and I could no longer manage my life enough to teach.

Many of my students pleaded with me to continue but I couldn't. I was incapable of any form of responsibility. After a couple of years I decided to pack up and leave Cordoba and make for the Costa del Sol, where I had been once before on holiday. Due to her family commitments, Inma could not make such a decision so easily. She stayed behind until I could 'spy out the land' for job possibilities.

I am aware that, like a well-chosen stone thrown carefully will bounce across the surface of the water, it may seem that I have selected a few incidents that skim across the surface of my life and barely touch it. However, please know that all of the incidents mentioned in this book were deeply significant both at the time they happened and in the profound way that they shaped my life for the future.

I loved my time in Spain especially these early years. Like a sponge, I soaked-in the culture, the music, the dance, the language, the history, the colours, the flavours....all that genuinely is authentic Spain. I had learned, in Alcoholics Anonymous, the folly of 'geographical change'. Unless we confront and deal with our problems that dwell within us, we will simply take them with us wherever we go. Time after time I tripped over the same obstacle. It was the demon of addiction. My battle had been a long one of transitory victories and crushing defeats. I was careering head first and out of control down a slippery slope into a looming chasm of foreboding darkness. Despite what I should have learned from life's lessons, I ignored any advice, warnings, my conscience or even my instincts. Amazingly, against all odds, help was on its way even although I still couldn't see it, or chose not to!

I started work 'touting' for a British bar in La Carihuela, near Torremolinos. I now spoke fluent Spanish so I was able to fill the busy bar with Spanish youngsters. For this I was paid a pittance, but I could drink as much as I wanted. That is, until the owners told me that I drank more than a bottle of brandy each night and had to cut back.

I met some people who explained some things to me about the 'Time Share Scam'. There were many elements to this, however, one of the parts that I could play was to get people out to the time share resort as early as possible. A bus would pick them up from a central location. If I could get couples there before a certain time the person who dealt with them at the Time Share Resort received a bonus that he or she would pass on to me. It may have been a bottle of whiskey, a meal in a restaurant, tickets for a tour, etc.... I could sell these 'bonuses' and make some money. Often I would go with a woman who would be my 'partner' for the sake of a day out and I would earn the early morning bonus. All she had to remember was to say 'no' and not buckle under the Time Share salesman's persuasive powers. In time, I became too well known in all the Costa developments to be able to work the scam any more.

Inma finally joined me and found work as a chambermaid in a nearby hotel. We rented a nice apartment in town with a swimming pool. My drinking was now completely out of control and I was also supplementing this with pills and 'soft drugs'. I had again lost the plot.

I still loved Inma, but I was too far gone to keep our relationship together. I had begun to live more and more in the twilight zone of drugs and alcohol. I made a brief journey to Gibraltar to find work, unsuccessfully, and also another trip to Spanish Ceuta

(North Africa). During that time there was some trouble brewing in the Middle East (1988/89) and everyone was leaving for fear of American reprisals. It was the preliminary stages of the Gulf War and I was promptly turned around at the African border and sent packing back to Spain.

One of the businessmen on the British strip of the now dubbed, Costa del Crime, was a drug smuggler. I found myself back in Morocco, North Africa, in the Rif Mountains, swallowing thumb-size pieces of cling-film-wrapped cannabis for exportation, in my stomach, to France for sale.... I became a drug smuggling 'camel'. The money I made for doing this, I lost when I was drunk in a bar on my first night back on La Costa. Inma was now working in a nightclub, learning how to cuss in English and how to drink like a fish. Meanwhile, I schemed and scammed for a living anyway I could.

I started sleeping rough on the beach or anywhere I could. This meant that I had to be up and about at first light to avoid the police. As soon as I woke up I needed a drink, but most of the bars were still closed. I used to follow the bread delivery van around and take out one or two loaves from each delivery that he left tied to café doors. When I had amassed enough bread, I made it back to the part of town where I was known. I bartered bread in the bars for brandy or beer. This gave me enough 'fuel' to start me in motion for another day of ducking and diving. However, time was running out, my credit had been used up. Most people were fed-up with Peter, the beach bum drunk.

One time, sitting in the forecourt of a little bar just outside the tourist strip, a 'friend' and I ordered a bottle of chilled white wine. When the bill came it was clear that we had been charged tourist prices and an argument broke out. In the heat of it I pulled out the folded parasol that went through the centre of our table and I attacked the bar owner with the pointed end. Fortunately, no real damage was done, a little scratch on the side of his head, but it could so easily have been much, much worse. He pressed charges but the police did not catch up with me until a long while later. I had to appear in court in Cordoba where I was then living. By the grace of God I avoided a jail sentence.

Despite all of my bad behaviour and reckless lifestyle, from time-to-time strangers would come up to me and say, 'You're a Christian, aren't you?' I guess, because they were Christians, they could see something that I couldn't. I was running away from Christianity but Jesus wasn't letting me go. On several occasions, while sleeping on the beach in wintertime, I would waken in the morning with a blanket over me. It may have been well-wishers, it may have been angels, but when all is said and done, it was Jesus. He still lived in my heart and He cared for me.

Quite possibly in the epicentre of a full-blown nervous breakdown, I decided that it was time to continue with my journey that had started when I ran away from Scotland in 1986. It was now some time in 1988/89. I made my way back to Morocco, North Africa. This time I headed south to Marrakech., the 'elephant's graveyard' for old hippies.

Be strong and courageous. Do not be afraid or terrified because of them, for the LORD your God goes with you; he will never leave you nor forsake you. (Deuteronomy 31:6)

8

NORTH AFRICAN MADNESS

After all the years of hitch-hiking, I guess I must have reckoned myself a 'seasoned' traveller, but nothing had prepared me for the culture shock that awaited me. I don't remember much of my train journey south. I do remember my arrival in Marrakech. Coming out of the station I was accosted by two young 'guides' and they would not let me go. They led me up narrow alleyways, down side streets and eventually into the main square, Djemaa el Fna, a bustling market place surrounded by cafes and bazaars. They left me dizzy outside a mint tea café, reeling from an overwhelming violation of my senses and sensibilities.

I couldn't understand a word of what was being spoken or anything that was written around me. I felt fearful and vulnerable. Somehow, I communicated my need for accommodation and I next found myself entering through a narrow door into a private courtyard. The first thing I saw was an ancient, wrinkle-faced man, down on his knees on a little colourful mat, bowing in prayer. A pleasantly jovial middle-aged woman showed me to a room. It was whitewashed, had a little bed, another small mat and a bare light bulb. I dumped my backpack down on the bed. It containing all I possessed in the world. I sat beside it and tried to make sense of what on earth was happening. I was terribly confused.

I remember thinking that I needed money and hit upon the idea of selling the contents of my back pack. I had a pair of trousers, a jumper, a t-shirt and a good waterproof and a pair of boots. I discovered (don't ask me how!) that a few doors away lived a man who would buy what I had to sell (he still reminds me of the seedy fez-donned trader played by Sydney Greenstreet in the movie 'Casablanca'). In my confusion I mixed up the exchange rate and sold everything for a tenth of what I meant to. A different young man followed me out of that house, showing an interest in also buying something from me. He offered a live chicken, which I refused, and then proceeded to barter with some cannabis resin scraped onto the inside of a semi-opaque plastic bag. I took it.

Back in my little room I was paralysed with anxiety and paranoia so I began to make joints and smoke the cannabis resin, quickly getting very stoned. The resin was extremely strong. Next thing I knew, the door to my room burst open and some policemen came in. They quickly bundled together what belongings I still had and threw me out on the street. They told me I must leave Marrakech.

I arrived at the train station to discover I had hardly any money. I couldn't afford the ticket back to Tangier. I remember the folk in the ticket office laughing and mocking me. Eventually I managed to purchase a cheap ticket that allowed me to travel with the natives and their livestock. On the train I nervously smoked more resin. I began to feel sleepy and lay down on top of the wooden-slatted bench seat and closed my eyes…

'Look at the state of him!'
I sprang up at the sound of voices
'Who does he think he is?'

These voices were familiar. Through the train carriage came a parade of familiar faces, yet they were wearing disguises. Some tried to make me laugh, others threatened me. I sat rigidly, staring straight ahead, somehow managing to direct air into my body, so that it became hard as steel.
'Even if we shot him now, the bullet would bounce off him. Look at his body!' one of them said.

I realised my hallucinogenic companions were people I had known from La Costa - bar owners, crooks, folk that I had thought had liked me and others that I knew didn't.

9

CONFRONTATION

The train slowed down, or seemed to. Actually, my carriage had been unhitched and directed into a siding. I tried to get off and run for it when I felt a thud on my thigh and a needle go in. My world went black.

When I came to, I was in a bare room with no windows. The door opened when I tried it and when I walked out I saw an African man sitting uninterestedly at the end of the corridor. I walked in the opposite direction and he didn't seem to bother. Outside, I discovered that I had been in one of a series of underground buildings. I walked around in the fields and found a perimeter fence of barbed wire. I was still pretty groggy and the fence started spinning around me . . ..

When I came round I was still in the field. I examined the fence for breaks and managed to get through it, only to be picked up within minutes by a Landrover and brought back into the compound. Another thud into my thigh sent me back to oblivion.

Days and days passed, so many I lost track. Apparently, the folk on the Costa mistakenly thought I had information about connections that would lead them to a huge drugs haul because of my previous involvement with trafficking. Why else would I be of such interest to anyone?

Eventually, I did manage to escape, or maybe they let me go in order to follow me. I found my way to a nearby town called Ksar el Kebir. I was in the Rif Mountains of Morocco. My leg hurt from all the injections; I kept falling down. At one point I had overheard a conversation, 'We'd better not give him any more.

We could kill him.' Another voice responded, 'He's a stinking junkie, he's used to it.'

I made my way around the town, looking for help. I was completely paranoid and disorientated. I thought I saw my captors around every corner. People kept chasing after me - just like in a bad film. At one point I remember being chased by different group who said they were after me. I found myself in an abandoned building that looked like a cinema from the outside. Inside sat a small group of people and I joined them. Next thing I knew there was a violent outburst of shouting and the man next to me was shot in the head.

I managed to get away but I didn't know where to turn. I thought it was best to stay in busy places, so I sat down on some steps where there were lots of people around. A man started to speak to me. I was suspicious, but he seemed kind and offered to help me. My clothes were soiled and my jeans were torn and muddy from falling. He told me to follow him and led me into a souk area. Behind the bazaar we found a group of wizened Moroccans sitting in a circle smoking a hubba-bubba.

My 'friend' spoke to one of them. The man got up and pushed open the shutter of what looked like a lock-up. Inside were bolts of all kinds of fabrics. He found a roll of corduroy and quickly made me a pair of trousers. They were clean, but I could have managed to fit both of my legs into one trouser leg! My 'friend' then took me to his home.

It was a fairly modern western style flat and inside a young boy was sprawled out on the sofa. They spoke in Arabic for a while and then my 'friend' disappeared. He had gone up onto the flat roof where he kept birds and had killed two for a meal. I was his guest of honour. After eating, I went for a walk around the neighbourhood. When I circled back towards the house, I saw a primitive fire engine parked outside the house which was ablaze. It was destroyed by fire.

I freaked out and sprinted to get as far away as possible. I found a police station and asked for help ... all my belonging were long gone, including my passport. After hours of begging, I managed to convince the policeman-in-charge of my desperate situation. He said that I could sleep in their cell that night for my own safety. In the meantime, he told a young western officer to accompany me, like a bodyguard, until nightfall. We went to a roadside café, which looked quite respectable. We ordered mint tea and immediately the young man began to roll joints and smoke hash. Quickly he became stoned. So much for helping me!

I needed to visit the toilet and asked the officer to stand guard at the back door. He refused, saying he could see the door from where he sat. I went through the door and outside to urinate into a roughly cut hole in the 'latrine'. Above where I was standing was a vent from the main building and I could hear voices. 'He's out there,' someone said. 'We'll get him when he comes back in.'

I quickly concocted a plan to draw as much attention to myself as possible. I raced back into the café and began to pile up tables and chairs in front of me, boxing myself into a corner. I screamed at the top of my voice for help. The officer-in-charge from the police station eventually appeared and took me and his rookie back with him. The young officer, who was extremely stoned, was put into my cell to sleep it off until the morning. I was taken, with the sound of the stoned officer's threats trailing off into the distance, to a local 'protected' brothel to sleep there. I lay on top of the bed in my little cell-like room, smoked a cigarette and listened.

I could hear the girls giggling among themselves and the sound of two men's voices who must have been one end of the room on a little raised platform. Although everything took place in Arabic, I seemed to understand what they were saying. They were negotiating my sale and purchase!

I lay there all night with my door closed tight and, at first light, made my way round to the police station. The policeman-in-charge called in a Moroccan native wearing a uniform that was far too big for him and a cap that was sliding off his head. He had a two tooth smile. He was handed the keys to a Landrover and ordered to drive me to Rabat, to the British Consulate. We sped off, taking corners on two wheels and skidded to a halt at the bus depot in Ksar al Kebir. My driver signalled for me to get out and then sped away and left me. Fortunately, one of the bus drivers saw all of this and offered to help me.

Over the next two days he drove his bus and all his passengers to Tangier (not Rabat) and whenever we stopped he would buy me some food. Using the stamped document from the police station at Ksar al Kebir as a substitute for my passport, I was able to board the ferry back to Algeciras in Spain. In Algeciras I managed to beg some money to catch another bus up the coast and back to La Carihuela …

10

HIDING

I quickly picked up from where I had left off. For the next few weeks I schemed my way from drink to drink. I had to visit the British Consulate in Malaga. Since I had no passport, they re-stamped the document I had with a thirty day extension after which I had to leave Spain.

In one of the bars where I delivered bread, the owner gave me a challenge. 'Get me two black-market plane tickets back to the UK, one for me and the other for you. The money is in a glass on the gantry.' I managed to get him a ticket almost immediately, but mine was to take a little longer. Eventually, I found a flight to Manchester. I remember arriving around 2:00 a.m. with my 'official document' in tatters and a carrier bag containing a potato (don't ask me why!). I started hitch-hiking. A young man who worked in the airport stopped and, going out of his way, took me to my uncle's house in Upton, near Pontefract.

I stayed there for a few days and then made my way north to Glasgow. I stayed with my parents but my mind and my life were in pieces. I drank in the pub opposite their house and fell in with the wrong crowd. Before long, I was delivering stolen cars back down to England. (The two brothers who stole the cars and arranged the buyer died of a drugs overdose not long after this.) I was never a good criminal and on the second or third run, half drunk, I ran out of petrol on the A66 with snow all around, in the middle of nowhere in the middle of the night.

The police stopped to question me and I asked them for money for petrol. They directed me to a petrol station a little further down the road where they said it might be possible to barter. I exchanged five cassette tapes for £5.00 worth of petrol. Back on the road, the same policemen stopped me in their car. They were suspicious. They asked me to get out of the car and into theirs. They checked my driver's license, which was clean, much to their surprise. They eventually discovered that the car I was driving was stolen, even though we had changed the number plates. The clincher was the screwdriver in the broken ignition barrel with wires hanging out like multi-coloured spaghetti...

They took me to a local police station, where, after searching me, they found sixty log books for cars of all shapes, colours and sizes. The CID came down from Glasgow to take me back. I was put into the Craigie Street cells to go up to Court on the Monday. During all of this I felt an extraordinarily strange peace to the point where I think I freaked out the other guys in the cell!

The CID questioned me and found me a lawyer. The consensus was that I should expect four to seven years in jail. They went to visit my parents as I was of 'no fixed abode'. I discovered later that they explained to my dad that if he said I lived there it would go better for me. His response, they said, was 'I haven't got a son called Peter.'

Monday morning came and I was taken with loads of other guys to the basement of the Sheriff Court in Glasgow where we were packed like sardines into the 'cages'. My name was shouted and I went out in the same direction as I had seen others go. 'You're going the wrong way, follow me.' I turned around to see a police officer at a desk holding up a clear plastic bag containing a 2 pence piece and a packet of cigarette papers.

'You're free to go', he said.
My mouth fell open, 'It's a trick' I thought.
'PF (Procurator Fiscals) release'.

I went through a door that led me straight outside. I was convinced it was a set up, because I was guilty. Surely they had released me so that I would lead them to the rest of the gang. 'I better stay well away.' I thought and accordingly, I found a bed-sit and went into hiding. I was miserable! I drank too much and grew steadily more paranoid.

11

FROM BAD TO WORSE

One night I was in a taxi and I noticed the driver 'clocking' me in his rear-view mirror.

'Are you Peter Stanway?' he asked.

Fear and sweats came over me. Surely he could smell it. 'Who wants to know?'

'You don't remember me, do you?'

'Uh ...'

'I'm John. You took my wedding photographs.'

'Oh!... yes.' I said, not remembering.

'Do you still take photos?'

'Not much.'

'I've got a job to drive a prototype off-road vehicle down to the Sahara Desert and back and the company are looking for someone to make a promotional video. Are you interested?'

Here was my emergency exit from Scotland. 'Sounds great.'

'I'll set up an interview.'

A short time later, I went down with John to Salisbury where, after a brief interview, I was given arms-full of state-of-the-art photography and movie cameras. We went to the tank testing grounds at Salisbury to put the vehicle and the equipment through their paces. The prototype was amazing, six wheels, a collaboration of Mercedes and Daimler. It was built for two couples, with a pop-up tent in the roof. There was a high-tech editing suite on board and super efficient alarm system. I found myself a token partner, a girl I vaguely knew, and together with John and his wife, we set off bound for the Algerian Sahara.

It rained all though France, so this made for good 'splashy puddle' shots. I drank my way through a case of red wine.

Southern France/Northern Spain and 'Los Picos de Europa'…. A dramatic broken teeth mountain range, covered in snow. John showed off his expertise as a rally driver and, communicating with me by walkie-talkie from different ridges, he put the vehicle through its paces. I managed to capture some good footage and stills.

Southward, and we pulled up outside the strip of bars I had spent so much time in just a few months before. It was like a triumphal return. We drove onwards to Algeciras to catch the ferry to North Africa. We decided to go for a meal and, since we parked in a busy town centre car park, we locked up, but didn't switch on the alarm. When we returned we had been robbed. A small trained monkey had been let through a quarter-light window and opened the doors from the inside. All the camera equipment was stolen. The mission was off and the game was up.

Having escaped from Glasgow again, there was no way I was going back. I got dropped off in La Carihuela and my new 'girlfriend' decided to join me. I was back 'touting' outside the Scot's Bar. For one or two nights I noticed a respectable looking man sitting watching me. He hardly drank. The next night he turned up in an open jeep and told me to get in. 'I'm working', I said. 'Get in, it's taken care of.'

We drove a short distance to the other side of Torremolinos and stopped outside a large, dark, closed building. We were met by a Spanish businessman.
'Translate for us' said the stranger from the bar. We went into the building, an un-used multi-purpose complex with a restaurant and night club. There was a roof-top swimming pool. Trevor, the stranger, was negotiating to buy it.

'What do you think?' he asked me.
'If it was full of people it would be amazing.' I replied.
'Do you want it?' he asked. 'You could run it for me.'

Wow, I thought, but in my heart I knew I couldn't do it. I wasn't able to cope with responsibility and I was dependant on huge amounts of alcohol and drugs. Trevor told me to think about it and to visit him the next day. He gave me the name of a small café where he would be. When I met him there he introduced me to his white wife and his black wife, one on each arm. He asked me if I needed any money and thrust his hand into a carrier bag full of notes of different currencies. He pulled out a wad and thrust them into my hands. He did this again on several other occasions. Depending on the currency, he gave me a few hundred pounds or hardly anything – it was money laundering.

Trevor showed up when he needed a translator, which was fairly regularly. I remember a time when he was buying a house in the hills for the boys from the UK to cool off after a job. It was mid-summer and I was sweltering in the car. Trevor and the other man sat at the poolside talking. From the car, I indicated that I would like to go for a swim in the pool. The man said it was okay. I took off all my clothes and dived in. As my head broke the water I was staring down the barrels of a shotgun. 'Get off my land!' Unknown to me, the man's wife was also at the poolside, shielded by her husband, I hadn't seen her. We were ordered off the land and told never to come back. I may have been a good translator, but I was a hopeless criminal!

I remember another time, sitting in the back of a big fancy car heading towards Marbella. The N10 was at that time the main route along the Costa del Sol. It was a busy and fast road. The Costa del Sol was (and is) a popular holiday destination for UK tourists. Often they would hire a car while on holiday and, unfamiliar with driving on the other side of the road coupled with much larger measures in the alcoholic drinks, they contributed regularly to the N10 having the worst record for road accidents and deaths in the whole of Spain. A consequence of this is that there was a lot of road-kill at the side of the road. Usually, it is so badly mangled that you cannot tell if it was a dog or a cat or something else that was killed.

As I Looked distractedly out of the car window I heard a voice speak to me. It was so audible that I thought, at first, it was someone in the car.....
'That's the way that you are going to end up; an unidentifiable bloody mess at the side of the road'.
It suddenly dawned on me that no-one knew anything about me, not even my second name. For a few seconds it was a sobering thought.

On another occasion we were driving in a big Mercedes car and it ran out of fuel. I was despatched with a Jerry can to get some. I came back and we filled up the car with petrol. Unfortunately, it should have been diesel. It was becoming clear that I wasn't cut out for this type of lifestyle. After this incident, that cost them a lot of money to sort out, I saw less and less of them.

I was soon back to my old ways, scrounging around the bars that would still allow me in. In one of these, desperate for a drink, I sat patiently waiting for the barman to be touched by my pitiful state. Suddenly, a drink appeared in front of me, the barman put a straw in it as I couldn't co-ordinate my simple motor movements to lift it to my mouth without spilling most of it. I guzzled it down and another one appeared. Quickly, I drank it. I asked where the drinks had come from and the barman pointed to a jovial looking little middle-aged English woman. I went over to talk to her and she bought me a few more drinks.

It transpired that she was lonely and was only looking for company. We went around together for a few days. It didn't take long for word to get to me that her husband, a convicted psychopath from London's East End, who had just been released from prison after fifteen years for manslaughter, was coming to Spain to find us and kill us. I was prepared to face up to him, but Margaret, his wife, jangled some money, like a carrot, in front of me and we caught a bus up into the hills to Mijas, a picturesque whitewashed little village with donkeys on the streets. Before too long the money ran out and I began to go through serious withdrawals. Wherever my eyes came to rest for more than a few seconds I hallucinated grotesque and frightening things. I began to vomit violently and I lost control of my body functions. I was in a terrible state. Margaret freaked out and said I had better get help. But where? I knew no-one in Mijas and I could not make myself function enough to scheme or scam. What could we do?

We were staying in a little 'pension', a small family-run hotel, and I knocked the door of the room next to us. A woman with an American accent answered and I asked her for help. She said her pastor might be able to help - my heart sank; 'Christians!', I thought. I had tried that and failed. Whenever anyone mentioned Church or Jesus it reminded me that I was a failure. How could I possibly go to God for help?

12

"I WANT YOU TO MEET SOMEONE"

By this time, Margaret, was frantic so I dragged myself along to our next door neighbour's church. The pastor answered the door, said he couldn't help and quickly shut the door in our faces. I though this was confirmation that God wasn't going to help..... However, unknown to me, just hours before, the same pastor, Roy, had been conned by some Scandinavian drifters. When he saw the way I looked (and smelled) he must have thought, 'Here we go again.' However, on our way to the church door we had passed the Sanctuary windows, where a prayer meeting was taking place. God had spoken to the group to pray for us and had said that a miracle would take place on Sunday.

Unaware of any for this, we went back to our room where circumstances became even worse. I had DT's (delirium tremens), serious withdrawal effects from drugs and alcohol. I was literally climbing the walls. Margaret could take no more; she dragged me to the Church the next day. I was stumbling and falling, coughing blood, shaking, sweating and full of anxiety. Brenda, the Pastor's wife opened the door. She had been part of the prayer group from the night before. Very kindly and full of grace she spoke to Margaret who had not eaten for days, since eating was not on my agenda and money was calculated in alcohol not food. Brenda gave her something to eat and took her into her home.

She told me that if I came back tomorrow there would be someone there who could help me. All I wanted was a few pesetas (now euros) for some wine and the bus fare back to the coast. The next day was dreadful. On top of everything else I had lost the power of my legs and, as I was soon was to discover, the power of my tongue too! I crawled that day to the church building, motivated by the possibility of being able to buy a bottle of wine. It was the third time and the third day of going to this church for help. This day was Sunday, but I didn't know that. There were people about and I just wanted to hide … I made my way into the Sanctuary. I was given the biggest warm-hearted welcome imaginable from the sweetest little grey-haired lady you ever saw. There were hundreds of people inside, so I quickly found a corner where I did my best go unnoticed.

The service started and folk began to sing in a language that I had never heard before. It sounded pure and clean – maybe like angels. Its loveliness magnified my ugliness and I felt debauched. I began to cry – 'Help!' Wee boys from Glasgow don't cry. I could not stop, yet strangely, the more I cried the cleaner I felt and the deeper this feeling went. Soon there was a puddle of tears that I could splash my feet in.

The next thing I knew I was in front of the whole congregation. I don't remember the sermon or any other singing. I was standing face to face with a pastor from a sister church. He asked me 'What do you want Jesus to do for you?' This was the same voice that I had heard on the N10 with reference to the road kill. What I heard was a loving, concerned voice asking me, 'What do you want me to do for you?' One word came into my mind, 'Everything!' Yet, I couldn't say it. I was like a dumb mute. I tried desperately to push the word out, going purple in the face trying to do so. Finally, it came out and I fell to the floor in a face-down heap. I thought I had passed out or fainted, as I had done many times before, but I was fully conscious of what was happening all around me.

There was shuffling of many feet … normally this would have filled me with fears, anxiety, paranoia, yet I had a feeling of peace. The congregation reached me; they began to touch me, laying their hands upon me. I realised that I felt security from their closeness and no longer was sweating or feeling sick. I opened my eyes and, since I was lying face down, I could see the back of my hand. It was beautiful! I could see all the little hairs, the pores and the freckles and it didn't change into something hideous or grotesque, there were no hallucinations. Emboldened, I looked up at the crowd. They were smiling and, as the sun came through the stained glass windows, it sent a splash of rich colour over the entire gathering. Real colour not imagined or drug induced.

I was conscious of getting stronger with every breath I took. Each inhalation seemed like I was breathing pure energy. I put my hands to the floor to push myself up. They were strong, not like jelly. Crouching now, I felt power flood into my legs. With a new confidence I began to stand up. Oh! The joy that overwhelmed me! Five feet, six feet, now seven feet, nine feet, ten feet tall – I felt like Superman. It was November 5th 1989 and, at long last, eighteen years after meeting Jesus Christ and God the Father, I now met the Holy Spirit.

My life would never be the same again. Sure, Brenda had asked me to come back to meet someone but I am sure neither she nor I could ever have imagined just who I was going to meet. The miracle that was prophesied three days earlier had taken place. Later that day I met the person that Brenda had arranged for me to see, June, and she took me home to have Sunday dinner with her and her family. I was ravenous! I ate mine and had second helpings too.

June was English. She had lived in Spain for more than twenty years, at that time, and was married to a Spaniard called Miguel. She had a good job in the best hotel in Mijas and was well respected by all. She introduced me to another ex-patriot who was going back to his homeland for a month who needed someone to house-sit, for that month, for him. I got the job.

Staying in a little self contained flat built into the ground floor of his sprawling Spanish villa, all I had to do was some basic maintenance, turn the lights on and off and pick leaves out of the swimming pool. What a turn around! The house was quite literally in the shadow of the church. Everyday, I was the first person at the church and the last away. I needed to understand what had happened to me. I even joined the choir just to be there. Before long, God started to speak to me from the Bible. He took me to 2 Corinthians 5:17: *Therefore, if anyone is in Christ, he is a new creation; the old has gone, the new has come!* Whoosh! These words went straight into my spirit. This is what had happened to me. I was a brand new person – the old was gone.

13

"KEEP THE DOOR OPEN"

The following month I found myself house-sitting for another expat. On the third month I was offered a house of my own by a couple who were moving from the house they had rented. The rent was paid-up for another two weeks. When I moved in I realised that the house was too big for me on my own. I began to walk around from room to room praying. In one of the bedrooms I knelt by a bedside with the open Bible before me. I felt led to read Matthew 25:35-40:

For I was hungry and you gave me something to eat, I was thirsty and you gave me something to drink, I was a stranger and you invited me in, I needed clothes and you clothed me, I was sick and you looked after me, I was in prison and you came to visit me. Then the righteous will answer him, 'Lord, when did we see you hungry and feed you, or thirsty and give you something to drink? When did we see you a stranger and invite you in, or needing clothes and clothe you? When did we see you sick or in prison and go to visit you?' The King will reply, 'I tell you the truth, whatever you did for one of the least of these brothers of mine, you did for me.'

Again I knew that God was talking to me. I heard the now familiar voice saying;
'I have been doing this for you for years. Now it's time you did it for others.' 'But how Lord?' I 'Just keep the door open and I'll do the rest.' At that very moment there was a knock at the door …
A boy from France stood there wide-eyed and bewildered;
'I don't know who you are, you don't know who I am but can you help me?' he pleaded. It was like looking at myself from just a few weeks before.

'Sure, come in!' I exclaimed. This started a multi-national flow of men who passed through the house over the next ten months. We could have ten to twelve people eating at any mealtime and up to fifteen staying in the house. Some folk would come for a meal, some for a month and others for a few months.

Most days, people would donate food or clothes to us. Soon we had two wardrobes full of clothes. Whenever anyone new arrived, they were able to have a shower or bath using donated toiletries and, with a towel wrapped around their waist, go to the wardrobe and pick out two sets of clean clothes. We would usually have to burn the clothes they arrived in! As I was still attending church at every opportunity, many of the men came with me. Virtually all of them gave their lives to Jesus, became Christians, and were healed.

Brenda had a 'deliverance ministry'. Apparently, she was really good at it as people from far and wide would come to her to be 'set free from demonic oppression'. When I had first started to attend the church I went through a few deliverance sessions with Brenda. If anyone needed to be set free from bad stuff it was me! However, as time went on, I began to notice that the same people were coming back week after week and month after month.

Sometimes Brenda would ask me to sit in on a session. Whether it was to learn, to watch, to assist, I don't quite know. I would see these same people go through the same antics time after time; screaming, writhing, being sick in a bucket and more. I discovered that some of these people had been coming to see Brenda for years. I began to think, 'surely they should be 'set free' by now?' It soon became apparent that some of them needed to be delivered from 'deliverance' more than they did from any demonic oppression. They enjoyed the theatrics and the attention.

In time, I came to understand that when a person is soundly saved at the cross of Jesus Christ and they surrender their life completely to Him, from that time onwards they are set free. The Bible, in the book of Galatians chapter five verse one says, *'It is for freedom that Christ has set us free'.* Often the 'freedom' issue centres around the question of whether or not the person was indeed soundly saved and did they surrender completely to the Lordship of Jesus Christ? I now know that without total surrender to Christ Jesus as Lord, there can never be absolute freedom.

After a couple of months of running the house and doing odd-jobs to pay the rent, word came to me that a 'psychopath from London' had turned up in the village and was looking for me. When I heard this I raced to the elders of the church to ask their advice.
'Let's pray about it.' They said calmly. Pretty soon they had the answer. 'You must go and talk with him!'
'What! This guy wants to kill me!!' However, in obedience, I plucked up the courage and went to see him. Miraculously, within a few minutes, he was slapping his thigh and roaring with laughter. It was as if we were long lost friends. He then confided in me that he had a problem. When he came to Spain the first time he went around all my old haunts saying, 'Where's this Scottish guy, Peter? I'm going to kill him.' As I had disappeared off the scene, people who knew me began to think he had done what he said. Soon the police became involved and he was deported from Spain on suspicion of murder!

Determined to get me, he arranged for some forged documents to be made and he was now back in Spain illegally.
'What will I do?' he asked me.
Before I had time to think, the Lord filled my mouth with these words, 'Come and stay at my house.' He did and, like the others, began coming to church with me. Within a week he had surrendered his life to Jesus and began his new life as a Christian.
He had a drawer full of prescribed medicine that he took; drugs for epilepsy, pain killers and sleeping pills. He came to me saying that he was healed and no longer needed them. Together we flushed them all down the toilet. Archie, my 'killer', was reconciled with his wife and they both returned to London.

One Sunday after church, a middle aged couple took me aside and asked me if I was free to come home with them. They had a surprise for me. They took me to their lovely home, parked their car and went to open the garage door. When the door opened, sitting in the middle of the garage floor was a shiny red Vespa 90cc scooter. My heart sank, my worst nightmare had come back to haunt me! I tried to mask my disappointment and thanked them profusely for their kind generosity. They gave me the keys and I drove it to the top of their steep driveway, stopped at the top of the hill, gently let the clutch out and vroom…the scooter shot forward and I remained standing, legs akimbo, like a cowboy without a horse. Picking up the scooter, I went back to see the couple, explained my story, gave them back the keys and said, 'thanks, but no thanks'.

Around this time my thoughts turned to my family back in Scotland. They would not have a clue what had happened to me and, judging from the way I was the last time they had seen me, they may even have thought that I was dead. I thought about how I could get in touch with them and properly explain what had happened. A letter would not quite do, even a cassette tape wouldn't fully paint the picture. Then it came to me; make a video. A couple in the church owned a good quality video camera so I decided simply to make a video diary over a typical weekend in my life. I made it and sent it to them. Technically it was full of faults but my heart came across correctly. Apparently, when she received it, my mother, who had indeed thought I was dead, watched the video VHS tape so often that she almost wore it out.

I watched that original tape much later and laughed so much that I almost fell off the sofa. Although it was hilarious and portrayed me like a bad B-movie actor as ham as a pork chop, it provides a fascinating insight into my life at that time. I couldn't believe how thin and gaunt, I was. At the end of the tape there's a clip of my water baptism in Roy and Brenda's sister church, built by Daniel del Vecchio, in Torremolinos. I deliberately wanted to be baptised in Torremolinos to give the devil a poke in the eye for the bad things that had happened to me when I lived there.

Some mornings, when we opened up the door of our house in Mijas, bags of food or farm produce left outside the door would fall into the house. On one occasion a box of purple cabbages tumbled in. Thanking God for his faithful provision, I began preparing them for the pot. I added them to the tomato based meal still in the pot and, once it was ready, we had a tasty, but die had come out of the cabbages creating a strange black sauce concoction. All of us had black lips and gums by the time we had finished eating! We had a good laugh at they way we all looked.

As time went by, we became more confident in God's ways. We could estimate how many would turn up for a meal according to the amount of food God supplied for the pot.
'How many do you think this will feed?' I asked the others. 'Ten' they agreed.
'How many places have we set at the table?'
'Eight' they replied.
'Better set two more places'. Sure enough before we ate, two more hungry guests would have arrived.

Early one morning as I was reading my bible and praying, the Spirit of God came upon me and I began to see a picture, like a movie, playing in my mind. I could see a place that I loved as a schoolboy, a 'secret place' that I would go to get away from everyone and everything. It was a tributary of the River Avon near Strathaven. A waterfall crashed down into the foaming river as it flowed into a deep, still pool. Trees stretched out their branches and, in season, their leaves caressed the water. In all seasons this was a magical place full mystery and beauty.

75

In the vision, the sun was shining high in the sky above the trees. Beams of light sliced through the shadows, like spotlights suspending flying insects in time and space. One of those beams highlighted a figure, dressed all in white, standing waist-deep in the pool. The contrast of his white raiment with the darkness around made him glow as though he himself was light. The waterfall behind him, much higher than I remember, was shrouded in a fine spray that caught the light and transformed it into a magnificent, ethereal rainbow like multi-coloured breath that was too delicate to capture.

This glowing figure beckoned me to come. I waded into the water and, as I approached, the figure skimmed his hand across the surface of the river sending water splashing all over me. I was taken aback and, instinctively, I splashed back. Immediately, our splashing developed into a full scale water fight. We were both laughing and drenched. We had a marvellous time; what joy and what elation. We were now within touching distance of each other and my beautiful friend put his hands together and cupped some water. He lifted it up above my head and poured it out upon me.

The water was amber in colour and it was thicker than water, more like oil. I could see the liquid run down his arms and spiral slowly from his elbows back into the water. He continued to cup this golden liquid and pour it over my head and, as he did so, my heart was pounding as though it would burst. I looked into his eyes and he smiled and I knew that he loved me. I was so thankful, so grateful. I became lost in the moment and then it was gone. I was back in my bedroom in my house in Mijas. I believe it was Jesus that I saw and the intimacy that we shared will remain with me forever.

Over the months our house became a home and, in that part of Southern Spain, it is traditional to have little domesticated, caged canaries that are put out on the balconies of Spanish homes to sing all day in the sun. I, and the boys in the house at that time, began to pray that God would give us a canary. We prayed for weeks but there was no canary. Then it dawned on us; how could God give us a canary if we had nowhere to keep it?

Around that time we had a visitor at the house, an English tourist who wanted to stay for a week. He had hired a car and wanted to take us out to do some sight-seeing. One day we drove to a town where some development work was going on. He parked the car behind a skip and as we were passing by it, there on top of the rubble was a discarded, beaten-up canary cage. We took it home, knocked it back into shape, cleaned it and fixed it to the wall with the door open. We continued to pray for a canary. One day in springtime one of the boys was walking up the steep hill from Fuengirola to Mijas. It's a steep climb and he had his head down with his body leaning into the incline. It had been raining and out of the corner of his eye he saw something splashing in a puddle. He bent down and saw a little featherless bird all but drowning in the shallow water. To save its life he picked it up and carefully tucked it into the inside of his jacket.

When he reached the house he told us what had happened and we all began to thank God for answering our prayer by giving us a canary. However, this little bird had no feathers and we had no way of knowing what kind it was. We carefully put it into the corner of the cage and began to look after it. Slowly, day by day, little fuzzy feathers began to grow on its tiny body. They were bright yellow; sure enough, it was our miracle canary.

On another occasion, we were all sitting around the dinner table but his time there was no food. The table was set with cutlery and glasses, jugs of water were at the centre, everything was in place, but no food. I began saying grace, giving thanks to God for his faithful provision. Then, as was our custom, the person next to me began thanking God in his own language also. We went round the table; German, French, Spanish … then back to me. I started again with even more gusto. There were some strange looks darting around the table and much shuffling of feet. The doorbell rang and everyone sprang up to answer it. There, standing in the doorway, were two French waiters, dressed in tuxedos and bow ties holding huge silver platters of cordon bleu French food. I invited them in, the others raced back to the table and the waiters served us one of the best meals that any of us had ever eaten. God is faithful.

A French boy who had lived with us had found a job in a French restaurant in another village. On this particular night a mistake had been made with an order. He caught them about to throw the food into the bin and told them about some folk in Mijas whom he knew could use the food and voila!.... another God ordained miracle.

14

FALL

During this time I was offered a job teaching English to Bank Managers in bank branches along the Costa del Sol. As the work progressed, and their trust in me grew, they gave me the keys to the front door so that I could go in and set-up the class before they came back for their lesson in the evening. How incredible is that? If they had only known that not long before I was negotiating for bank robbers to buy 'cool off' houses in the sierras that they could see from their office windows. Yet another example of God's amazing, transforming grace.

I was flying on eagles' wings for around eight months or so when the offer of a job came up in a language school in Marbella. We needed to generate some income for the house and it seemed like a good idea. The church in Mijas was looking to plant a church in Marbella and I was being prepared to, eventually, become the pastor of the new church so, this part-time job would give me an opportunity to get know Marbella and its people.

From the abundance of provisions for the house in Mijas, I thought that it would be good to take some sandwiches to the street people and homeless who hung around begging in Marbella. The trouble was that this was my 'unsanctified good idea', not a God-inspired idea, and it was to lead to disaster. I have learned, over time, only to do what God tells me.

I befriended a couple who were sleeping in a car, both of whom were heroin addicts. I had some lovely friends (Cyril and Breda) who had recently opened a drugs rehabilitation centre in a big rambling house, in the Malaga area. Up until that time they had never had anyone stay there, so they were delighted at my suggestion that Juan and Daniela should go there. Juan only lasted a couple of nights and was quickly back on the streets, sleeping in his car in Marbella. Daniela lasted longer and eventually kicked her habit.

After ten months since I first opened the door to the house in Mijas, I felt that it was time to pass the keys on to some of the boys who had been there from the beginning. I was getting busier in Marbella so it made sense to rent a flat there to cut down on commuter time and expenses. I found Juan sleeping in his car and invited him to come and stay at my flat. I was completely unprepared for what happened next. Like an eighteen-wheeler truck careering out of a side-street it hit me. Without any premeditation or even a thought, I ended up taking drugs with Juan. I was devastated. How could this have happened?

1 Corinthians 10:12 says: '*So, if you think you are standing firm, be careful that you don't fall!*' Oh boy, did I fall. I found myself in the centre of Malaga along with Juan (who had Aids) selling our blood to a donor bank. Since Juan was a registered drug-addict we went to a doctor in Malaga and worked some kind of scam for him to give us the most powerful prescribed drugs I have ever taken. The next thing I remember was falling all over the place, amidst crowds of people who were taking a wide berth to avoid me, as I tried to beg money outside the train station to buy a ticket back to Marbella.

I must have got there because when I woke up I was on the beach. I found the way back to my flat but I had lost the key. I kicked the door in and went inside. I was confused and very afraid. I needed help desperately but I couldn't face anyone that I knew. I couldn't go back to the language school and I certainly couldn't go near the church. I started going to Narcotics Anonymous and Alcoholics Anonymous meetings and met a few people who befriended me. I had no work now so, one of the men who attended the meetings offered me a job to paint and decorate his house and to do some odd jobs around the place where he lived. I did my best but I was far from right. My head was messed-up and I was finding it difficult to connect with reality. I was again, living in a twilight zone.

My mega-binge had lasted only one day but I was recoiling from it for many weeks afterwards. Winter was coming. I eventually made my way back along the coast to Fuengirola. I knew that I had to contact Roy and Brenda. I finally plucked up the courage to phone them and they said they would collect me in their car and take me back to the church. I waited, hiding near the pre-arranged meeting place, but when I saw their car I stayed hidden. Twice this happened over the next few days until I eventually went with them back up the hill to Mijas.

15

REHAB

Roy and Brenda did all they could to help me but I was like an insane person. They didn't know the person I had become and neither did I. I was out of control. Consequently, they phoned up a Rehab on the other side of the mountain from Mijas in a village called Alhaurin el Grande. There was a connection between the people there and myself owing to what was done at the Mijas house and also because of my involvement with the church in Mijas.

When I knew that I was going there I went to a local chemist and bought some legal sleeping pills over the counter. I had calculated how many I would need to sleep for three days because I reckoned that after three days my body would be over the worst of the physical detox. They put me in a bed in the bunkhouse dormitory and I took those pills every time I woke up for the next three days until they were finished, and I was finished.

They woke me up on the fourth day, gave me an axe and assigned me to chop logs for the fire. I was so shaky on my feet that it is a miracle that I didn't chop my leg off! It was the winter of 1990. I was to stay in rehabilitation almost continually for the next three-and-a-half years. That was probably the same amount of time that I would have served in jail, if it had not been for the PF (Procurator Fiscal's) release.

During this time, at that first-phase rehab in Alhaurin el Grande, I earned enough trust to go out as the 'van boy' to collect food that was being donated to us. One of the leaders drove and I went to lift and carry. The main source of income at the rehab centre was selling pigs. It was a pig farm and much of what we collected was food for the pigs. It wasn't bad and often one of the bonuses of being assigned to feeding the pigs was that you could eat the biscuits and cakes that they were eating!

We were all a bit rough and ready in the rehab. Everyone was Spanish except me, yet because of my love for all things Spanish I was probably more Spanish than the rest of them. I not only spoke Spanish all the time, I even dreamt in Spanish.

One day, one of the little piglets died (presumably of natural causes) and it was decided that we would eat it. None of us were butchers but one or two had used a knife before and they were assigned to prepare the pig. When I returned from my day away collecting food donations and went into the canteen I saw that a white sheet had been laid-out over the dissected pig and blood was coming through. This was somewhat of a distraction and I hardly noticed when the cooks came round offering the rare treat of a pig's ear until it was plopped-down on the plate of the boy next to me....a hairy, pink ear.

Hardly able to take my eyes off of that repugnant ear, I picked up some crusty bread to dip in my soup, took a bite and crunch! 'Oh no, that's another of my teeth away' I said to myself as I worked my tongue around my mouth to find the broken fragment...'What was this?' As I pulled a row of teeth from my mouth, I realised that I had spooned in part of the lower jaw bone of the piglet and, worse still, I then realised that the soup we were eating was made from it's entire head!

Talking about 'entire heads'..... Occasionally the men from the rehab would reach out with the love of God to people who had problems in the village. In doing this, there was a time when they had come across a boy who had never left his house in over three years. Not only that, but he had never left the room where they found him. He never even visited the toilet simply using the room he was in to do his needs. Apart from one or two infrequent visitors he was alone.

Strewn around him were soiled newspapers, discarded food wrappers, dead flies and the smell. He had sat on the floor allowing his hair to grow until it hung over his entire face. He could not see out and no-one could see his face. Antonio, the recluse, was talked into coming to the rehab for help and I befriended him. Over weeks of unthreatening conversation and loads of TLC, Antonio eventually permitted me to cut his hair. What a difference that made to his appearance but it also made Antonio feel vulnerable and exposed. There was now nowhere for him to hide; being around him called for super-sensitivity. One day upon returning from a food run I discovered Antonio was gone. At lunch, one of the new boys had made a joke at his expense and Antonio had lunged at him with a fork to stab him in the eye. He was subdued but later escaped. I never saw him again.

As time went on I was allowed to go outside to do contracted work for which the Rehab was paid. One job that I had and loved was making drainage tunnels that conducted water from the mountain streams to run under the roads. This was to prevent them from being washed away when the streams became raging torrents in spate in the wintertime. We were high up in the mountains. The experts put in the ten feet diameter pipes but we labourers had to build the wall around the mouth of the pipes where they came out from under the road. Sometimes these walls could be fifty feet high and thirty feet wide. They were like giant dry stone dykes except that every stone was cemented in place. There was a real sense of freedom up there with eagles flying around and in the company of hard-working healthy men in the real world.

One day, after working hard in the mountains, I returned to the rehab to find everyone gathered together in a large circle in the open air listening intently to someone speaking that I had never seen before.

16

THE FARM

I had no sooner joined the group when this stranger addressed me in English. I was taken aback and had to think about what he had said.

'Pack your belongings, you're coming with me.'

'Where I am I going?' I asked.

'Antequera, to the big farm. I need a hand with the harvest'

It turned out that this 'stranger' was none other than Daniel del Vecchio, the person responsible for starting the rehab at Alhaurin el Grande and, I later discovered, he had also physically built the church buildings in Mijas and Torremolinos and established the substantial farm (finca) at Antequera where REMAR ('Rehabilitación de Marginados'/ Rehabibilation of Marginalised People) was started.

Daniel was an apostle of Italian/American extraction and a bricklayer to trade. He arrived in Malaga, Spain in the 1960's to knock on doors and evangelise. Through a series of divine opportunities, he was given a one-hundred bedroom hotel in Torremolinos to use to help hippie 'casualties' who got lost on the 'Michener Trail'; a hippie hybrid of physical and fantasy journeys from Amsterdam to Marrakech based on *The Drifters* by James Michener.

In time, Daniel added to his vision the Finca at Antequerra - a huge dairy farm of more than one-hundred-and-fifty champion high-yield dairy cows and acres of sweet corn or maize that Daniel pioneered as food for people, rather than animal fodder, throughout southern Spain. He was known as King Corn. Antequera was just off the main road about one third of the way towards Cordoba from Malaga.

Daniel came to fetch me from Alhaurin el Grande to take me to the second-phase rehab at Antequera. Here his Christian disciples were expected to make a commitment of between eight and fifteen years of service. In total there were never more than eight men living there five of whom were going through rehab and doing most of the physical hard work.

The first job I had to do was build a giant hay stack of twenty-three thousand bales of hay. It was like a skyscraper tower block lying on its side. We had no sooner finished this when, in the intense heat of mid-summer, it internally combusted and burst into flames. Five fire engines came and spread the haystack out over all the surrounding fields and it took almost two months for it to stop burning.

However, the cows still needed bedding for the winter and another hay stack had to be built. This time it was only eighteen thousand bales! While all this was going on, the cows still had to be milked, fed and cleaned. The cows were herded into the barn and milked in rota four times a day from dawn to dusk. The milking was done with special milking equipment and fed directly into a large refrigerated vat where it was collect every day by the milk tanker. The milk was so creamy that we were rationed to one cupful per day.

After building the second hay stack it was time to harvest the sweet corn (corn-on-the-cob) and package them for sale in the markets and shops all over Andalusia. Once the eight foot stalks had been harvested we had to go round with a scythe and cut them down. They were collected in rows and fed into a shredder that turned them into pulp that was to become like caviar for the cows in winter. This pulp was spread by the tractor into a three-sided silage area and the five of us had to walk with our heels to the walls, where the tractor couldn't go, and compress it with our body weight. We had to do this with every fresh layer of pulp, scattering a fermenting agent between layers. The job had to be finished in one go and it took sevent-two hours to complete.

Over time, I learned a lot about the rhythm of nature and many of Jesus' parables came alive to me while I lived on the farm. I was there for one full agricultural year.

Don't let anyone tell you that chickens are stupid. There was a chicken coop on the farm with about one hundred chickens. It was looked after by a boy with special needs. Daniel decided that there was no profit in chickens and he decided to sell them. One day a blue transit van came to take them all away. I watched as they chased and corralled them all into the back of the van. When it got down to the last few it was more difficult to catch them.

Finally, there were two chickens left. They looked a sorry sight; one was dragging its wing on the ground and the other was liming with a bad foot. Their buyer couldn't be bothered trying to round them up. They looked so pathetic that he decided to leave them behind. He closed the back doors of his van and drove off. He wasn't even off the farm when the rejected birds gave themselves a shake, stretched their necks and ruffled their feathers. There was nothing wrong with them at all. I watched them strutting around the yard, I'm sure I saw them smiling....

It was extremely hard work on the farm and it wasn't easy, especially in the beginning. When it came to the time to fertilize the fields they used slurry from the cow manure to plough into the fields. This had been collecting for a while in the dung trough in the milking shed. It was washed in there with a high-power hose after every milking. The tractor had a large vacuum tube to suck the slurry into a tank it towed, but the tube couldn't get it all. I was given the job of jumping into the dung trough with plastic waders up to my chest and with a long-handled squeegee, I pushed the liquid dung towards the tube.

One night, not long after I moved to the farm, I sneaked out late at night and under the cover of darkness I made my way to the farthest corner of the fields and I screamed until I was hoarse; until the knot in my stomach went away.

Daniel was a builder both of people and buildings. He had some land in the city of Malaga and he wanted to build a church there. Scribbling away on pieces of paper, he frustratedly threw them into the corner of his office. In walked Andy one day. He was a mathematics drop-out and former 'casualty' from Torremolinos;
'What are you doing Daniel?' He asked.
'I am trying to design a new sanctuary for Malaga.' Daniel replied.
'That's it!' said Andy, pointing to the heap of crumpled, discarded sketches in the corner. 'I could design that for you.'
They set to work and came up with a quarter-sized prototype that they built on the farm. It was perfect. It looked just like a giant golf ball with every dimple a unique shape made from semi-opaque fibre glass.

Soon after that, The Tabernacle was built on Daniel's land in Malaga and, with three aisles leading into the perfectly acoustic dome, it could seat in excess of two thousand people. So good were the acoustics that the speaker on the podium at the centre of the dome did not even need any amplification.

It was the job of the Pastor who lived on the farm with his wife and children to sell the sweet corn. He chose me to go with him to help with the lifting and hauling. I saw what he did and how he did it. It wasn't easy to convince shop managers to take a few trays to try. I guess it must have been a similar scenario as trying to promote organic food when it was first introduced into the supermarkets.

After a few weeks, Pastor Marco and his family went on holiday leaving me to supply the corn-on-the-cob to existing customers and try, if I could, to get some new customers. God was with me and I did very well bringing-in a sizeable revenue during the time the pastor was away. I thought he would have been pleased with me when he returned but, instead, he was furious. Even to this day I don't know why. That night, frustrated and angry, I stole one of the little vans from the farm and drove to Cordoba. I went straight to Inma's house.

17

DECEPTION

I was amazed. Since I had last seen her, Inma had given her life to Jesus and become a born again Christian. I was delighted for her but it meant that I couldn't stay there. She spoke with her pastor, Esteban, who found me a place to stay for the night. The next day, after quizzing me about what had happened, he made arrangements for me to return the stolen van. He followed me back to Antequera in his car, saw me hand over the keys and apologise then drove me back to Cordoba.

Things were not good. In fact, I was in a mess and Pastor Esteban could see this. He recommended that I stop seeing Inma and that was the beginning of the end of my relationship with her. I ended up in hospital, in a locked psychiatric ward. It was awful. I was given lots of strong medication that didn't help at all. After a week to ten days I was discharged with the recommendation that I attended an alcohol unit for recovering alcoholics. I did. This time it was all men who were chronic alcoholics and many were dying with cirrhosis of the liver or other alcohol related illnesses. I was put on medication that made me rapidly lose weight and my muscles wasted way.

I met some fascinating people in there. One was an ex-Legionnaire, Henri, from the days when the Foreign Legion was a regiment of reprobate criminals on the run from justice. He told me that when you enlisted you were given two squares of linen cloth. These were your socks and, years later, if you ever wanted to leave, these two squares had to be handed-in intact with no holes in them. That meant that these tough men had to wash them and darn them regularly. These hardened criminals had to learn responsibility. They were also taught to eat anything and everything. I remember sitting at his table in the refectory at the unit when we were given custard apples as a desert. These fruits are soft on the inside but have tough, leathery skins with seeds as hard as pebbles about the size of kidney beans. Henri ate everything, the inside, the outside and all the seeds, he cleared his plate. Nothing went to waste, he was a survivor.

Don Pedro, who ran the unit, was a good and well respected man. He did a tremendous job. After a while I was allowed to come and go as I pleased. It was around this time that the law caught up with me from the fracas over the bottle of wine on the Costa, when I had used the large parasol as a weapon. I had to appear in court in Cordoba. I apologised to the bar owner who was there and background reports from Don Pedro and his team were submitted. Miraculously the case was dismissed.

When I was at Daniel's farm I had begun drawing again and strangely enough the gift was still there. Encouraged by an artist, Juan Zivico who attended Don Pedro's alcohol unit, I began to paint. When I was out for the day I would often visit Juan in his studio in the city. He was a renowned international artist. Juan helped me to get a job as a darkroom assistant for students who were doing a photography course run by the town council. I was able to develop and print a series of photographs I had taken of a gypsy family that I had befriended. My photos became part of an art exhibition in Cordoba city centre.

Juan had planned a major art event in one of the large public parks in Cordoba. It involved three groups of youths, whom Juan had been teaching, all simultaneously painting three mural size canvases (twelve feet x ten feet) live. The press were there and a large crowd gathered. Unfortunately, all of the artists took 'stage fright' and were paralysed with fear. I jumped in and, in a creative frenzy, began to throw paint around on these huge canvases. I gave brushes and paint to the gathered spectators and soon they too were getting involved, as was originally planned. It was a great, messy and colourful event that all of us, including the now participating 'scared' youths, thoroughly enjoyed.

Encouraged by Juan, I soon had a large air-conditioned studio to work in courtesy of the town council. Before long, I was being introduced to mayors who began inviting me to exhibit in their towns. I was sure this was of God. My first one-man show was in a town called La Victoria (The Victory) and the second was in a town called La Conquista (The Conquest). Pretty soon radio, television and newspaper reviews and interviews followed and I was invited to exhibit in a gallery in central Cordoba. Tragically, it turned out that I was deceived. None of this was of God, but rather, of my own making; another series of 'unsanctified good ideas' and, without warning, I came crashing back to reality.

18

HOME

Despite the fact that I was taking Antabuse, a medicine that causes violent vomiting and heart palpations if mixed with alcohol, I decided to go for a drink in Cordoba. I didn't drink much, just a couple of glasses of wine but the symptoms started immediately. By the time I made it back to Don Pedro's alcohol unit I thought I was going to die. They knew what to do immediately and a nurse there injected me with the antidote.

After this episode, my days at the clinic were numbered and I clearly saw the writing on the wall. I found a job selling religious calendars around the doors. The company would pick a group of us up very early in the morning in central Cordoba and drive us to the towns and villages where we would go door-to-door selling. At the end of the day we would all meet together and be taken to our bunkhouse accommodation to eat and sleep. We would repeat this process for two or three days until all the calendars were sold.

I did this for a couple of days and, at the same time, I started drinking again. I bought a bottle of wine and drank it throughout the day. It didn't stop me from being able to sell my wares and, at the end of the day, I had sold quite a number of calendars. Instead of meeting up with the others I decided I would keep the money and make my way to Mijas.

When I eventually arrived there I found June and asked her to help me. Throughout all my time since first arriving in Mijas, June had been a tremendous help to me. She picked me up when I fell down and she encouraged me. She came to my exhibitions in Cordoba. She was the manifestation of God's love for me. However, even to June, it was becoming clear that my time in Spain was coming to an end. I had overstayed my welcome and I knew it. I loved Spain and didn't want to leave but I couldn't go on like this. I stayed on for as long as I could in a dingy little room that June had found for free for me. I consumed enough alcohol to block out reality and avoided contact with people and the church. I was back in the twilight zone and it was becoming very scary again.

June managed to find the contact details for a rehab back in England and arranged a place for me. All I had to do was call them from Gatwick Airport when I arrived there. It was now January 1993. I arrived at Gatwick clutching a bottle of whiskey. I managed to make the phone call, and fell asleep in the waiting area. Mike arrived, gave me a shake, and told me to follow him to the van. He drove me to Spirit and Word in High Wycombe. He put me in an attic bedroom and that's where I stayed until the shaking stopped. By the grace of God, that was the last time that I ever drank alcohol or took drugs.

As you can imagine, it took me a while to adjust to the culture of England. Every day I would attend a rehab centre in town. There were bible studies and recreational activities and some physical work to do. Day by day I became more adjusted and stronger.

While I was at Spirit and Word I stopped smoking cigarettes and I have never smoked since. I was feeling strongly convicted and guilty about smoking. I wanted to get right with God and I knew that sneaking away for a 'fag' at church was wrong. It was like lying to myself and others. I was aware that everyone knew that I smoked because I smelled of it. It all came to a head one day and I told everyone in the rehab house that the next day I was stopping.

I told them that I would stay locked in my bedroom for as long as it took to get over withdrawals. I asked them to lock me in at bedtime. I reckoned it would take about three days based on my previous detoxing experiences. That night I smoked all my tobacco before going to bed. The next morning I awoke bright and breezy with no desire to have a roll-up (a make-your-own cigarette). As the morning wore on no cravings came so, I shouted through the locked door that I was ready to come out of the room. They laughed at me and told me that they weren't falling for that old trick....

This experience of stopping smoking was to be, for me, a profound lesson in life and a key to overcoming any addictions. I realised that in my heart, the night before, I had truly quit smoking. There was none of me that wanted to continue and, because of that resolve, that one-hundred percent determination, the battle was won and I had quit. It took me all of that day and into the evening before I could convince the other guys in the house. Around nine o'clock in the evening they finally unlocked the door. The lesson that I learned, and have been able to use when working with addicts over the course of my life, is profoundly simple; unless a person truly wants to quit what they are doing, unless they want 100% to stop, they will not succeed. If there is the tiniest part of them that wants to continue in the old ways then that fraction of a percentage will become their 'Achilles' heel'. It becomes the access point through which the enemy, the spirit of addiction, will come in and destroy that person's life.

Nowhere is perfect and Spirit and Word had its fair share of faults, not least the fact that it was defrauding the DHSS. They were making false claims for residents who unwittingly signed their carefully folded giros to validate the claim that was made in their name. They were caught and the owner Julie and her daughter Grace were imprisoned. Mike, Julie's son-in-law, who had collected me from Gatwick airport, ended-up a drug addict and was estranged from his wife Grace. One day he went berserk and went after her with a chainsaw. He was confused and distraught but no-one was injured. A court order meant that Mike was not allowed to come within half-a-mile of his home or to have any contact with his wife or child. Mike killed himself.

Sometimes people were referred to the rehab for a week or two by their GP. Billy, a Scotsman living in Norfolk, was one of them. He had an alcohol problem. While he was at Spirit and Word we got on well. After he left we hoped to keep in touch. As I began to grow in strength physically, I also began to grow stronger spiritually too. I read the Bible regularly and my mind was being renewed. Despite the unrighteous circumstances, I began to get right with God. One day it was announced that all of us were going to a Christian Summer Camp at the end of July. I enquired more and found out that it was called Faith Camp and was headed up by a man called Colin Urquhart. I knew a little about him from the books I read when I first attended the Mijas church. I began to look forward to going.

I decided, and made it plain, that after Faith Camp I would not return to High Wycombe with the others. God had spoken to me through the Bible and said, *'You have made your way around this hill country long enough; now turn north'* (Deuteronomy 2:3). I knew that God was sending me back to Scotland, but I wasn't ready for that – not yet. I had no idea what would happen after Faith Camp but I felt confident that God did know.

19

FAITH CAMP

Faith Camp was amazing. The main speaker that year (1993) was Ulf Ekman and I learned a lot from him but it was the worship that truly blew me away. I had never heard anything like this. Every evening I literally touched heaven. I was caught-up in the Spirit and had visions of angels and of Jesus. I couldn't get enough and I wanted more.

I asked around and discovered that Faith Camp came out of Kingdom Faith Ministries and their main base was at Roffey Place in West Sussex where they had a Bible College. They were giving interviews for the college at Camp. Nervously, I went along to have my interview with Director and Prophet, Bryan Spence. It was the weirdest interview I have ever had.

He sat side-on in a chair facing away from me. I moved my chair to look him in the eyes and he moved his chair to be side-on again. 'Fair enough', I thought. He stared straight ahead and coughed quietly while scratching his beard;
'So you think you should go to Bible College? He said. 'Has the Lord told you to go?'
'Yes', 'I believe so,' I replied to both questions.
More scratching and quiet coughing.....'OK, I think you should go. Do you have the money?' He asked.
'No'
'Do you believe you will have it before the end of the course?
'Yes'
'OK. Pay it before you finish'
And that was it. I was tentatively accepted to be a student at Kingdom Faith Bible College.

I fasted and prayed my way through the rest of that week and made sure I was at as many meetings as possible, especially the worship. One of the afternoon seminars was run by a Croatian woman called Gordana Toplak. She had appeared on the KF (Kingdom Faith) scene only weeks before. She was a graduate from Ulf Ekman's Bible College where she had studied in the School of Prayer under Mary-Alice Isleib. What I learned there was to radically influence my prayer life for ever. In fact, it was there that I learned what prayer is and how to pray.

The week was drawing to a close and I was on a high, a spiritual high like never before. I was changed, impacted by the experience of true worship and fervent prayer. I hadn't given my next move much thought when suddenly, Saturday morning arrived and it was time to dismantle the camp and leave. I had asked to be dropped-off at Peterborough train station (Faith Camp takes place at the East of England showground near Peterborough) and I was considering heading up to Scotland.

As I was packing-up, my attention was drawn to a crowd of laughing children. They were running after a slow-moving car that was being driven around the camp site. I looked closer, and laughed too, when I saw that the windscreen wipers had been pulled away from the windscreen. A glove had been placed on the end of each one and the wipers were switched on making it look like a pair of hands were waving from the bonnet of the car. When I went to inspect further, I saw that it was my friend Scottish Billy from Norfolk, who was looking for me. The Lord had spoken to him about coming to Faith Camp to fetch me and take me home to live with him and his family.

20

BIBLE COLLEGE

We arrived at Horsey on the edge of the beautiful Horsey Mere, a part of the Norfolk Broads made infamous by its windmill that was used to send coded signals to the smugglers when the coastguard was near. I was amazed by how small the village was (four houses and a phone box) but I was equally enthralled by the peace, tranquillity and loveliness of the whole area. It was only a short walk from the wild coastline of the North Sea and, I still had a soft spot for beaches where angels had sometimes attended me unawares back on the Costa del Sol.

Not only was Billy's village small but his house was also small and made even smaller by his five children, wife and mother who all lived there. I was also to be added to the mix. Cramped? You bet!

Billy had a business as a window cleaner but he had lost his licence due to drink-driving offences. He couldn't do his job (legally) and desperately needed a driver. I started to drive him around and quickly became familiar with his circuit of customers. Soon I was able to not only drive him but also to help him wash the windows. We became good at it, quite a formidable team. We managed to do the work quickly and that allowed us time to talk with the customers and, of course, evangelise.

Billy and his family attended Green Pastures Church in Caister, a small town nearby. Their Pastor, Colin King, was a farmer from Winterton. A few weeks after I arrived, the elders of the church saw the predicament we were all in and unanimously agreed to buy me a little caravan in which to sleep and study. It was the smallest caravan you have ever seen, I almost had to go outside to turn around! However, with the added awning, it was just what we all needed.

Colin offered me some work on the farm that I gladly accepted. We got to know each other very well and we have become lasting friends. One day Colin asked me if I would like to try my hand at ploughing with his big tractor. I explained that I had never done this before and he said it was easy. All I had to do was line up something on the landscape that wouldn't move, a tree for example, with something on the tractor like the wing mirror. I set off, determined to plough in a straight line. I did what Colin told me but the deep furrows of the field and the huge tyres of the tractor made it so bouncy that I had to look back to see if I had gone off-course.

It all looked okay, so I continued until the end of the field and did a one-hundred-and-eighty degrees turn to plough my way back to the other end of the field where I had started. Imagine my horror when I saw the great big wobbly furrow. I had gone off course but only when I looked back. What I great lesson I had learned; we have to keep our eyes focussed forward and not look back. If we look back we will 'wobble' and go off course in our life. *"No one who puts his hand to the plough and looks back is fit for service in the kingdom of God."* (Luke 9:62)

Pastor Colin liked Colin Urquhart's teaching and, therefore, he was all in favour of my going to Kingdom Faith Bible College. When the day came for me to have my formal interview at Roffey Place, Pastor Colin drove me there.

I was interviewed by Jonathon Croft, who became the Director of the Bible College, and he concurred that I should go to Bible College but not at Roffey. He suggested that I go to the new Kingdom Faith College that had just open in Northern Yorkshire; Lamplugh House in a little village called Thwing, (sounds more like a speech impediment than an actual place!). Jonathon said I should go there for one term only just to knock me into shape and recommended that I should go for the next semester starting in January 1994.

I was delighted and couldn't wait. I went back to Horsey with the good news. As the winter began to bite, and the north winds began to blow, it really began to hurt our frozen fingers when we were cleaning windows. Even although I was now living in Norfolk, among 'the folk of the north', and was heading for North Yorkshire, I knew deep in my heart that God was still telling me to 'make my way north' to my family in Scotland.

I felt that I should go to visit my family in Scotland for one night on the week before Christmas. Billy was furious because that was the big tips week. He reluctantly agreed to let me go. What a time of blessing it proved to be. Neither my family nor I knew what to expect. The last two times they had seen me at home I had run away on both occasions. The news they had received from me since then was sporadic at best and confusing. When I entered into my mother's living room there was a crowd waiting to see me. Three things struck me, firstly how old my mum looked (probably my fault), how fat the women were and how keen they were to hear my story. My mum was on the edge of her seat and could not wait to get saved. By the end of the night my sister and her husband and my mum all gave their lives to Jesus. It was a wonderful time. I felt at home and I felt loved by 'my ain folk'.

21

ANOINTING

Back down in Norfolk, we did manage to get the tips in and everyone had a great Christmas. As we entered into 1994 my thoughts turned towards Bible College and excitement began to well-up within me. When the day came to start, Pastor Colin King drove me all the way to College and came in with me. I was busy with registration and getting my bag in. I walked Colin back out to his car and gave him a huge hug and a big 'thank you'. I went back into see Shirley, the college Administrator, and she told me that Colin had just paid one-third of my course fees for the semester. I was deeply touched. The church had gathered an offering for me and Colin had paid the money without me knowing it.

Over the next twelve weeks all my fees would be paid, mostly by people I didn't even know – anonymous donations. It was a great testimony of faith for Bryan (the Director), Shirley and me. I remember once a cheque for £50 came in made out to Peter Stanway. Since I didn't have a bank account, I had to write back to the donators to thank them and to ask them to write another cheque this time made out to the college. They wrote back to me to thank me for sending the cheque back since they had hardly slept a wink since sending it. They went on to say that they had been disobedient to God in what they had given me and re-issued a new cheque, made out to the college, for the amount that God told them to give, £168.75. Amazing....

I was only going to be there for one semester lasting twelve weeks and I was going to make it count. I spent most of my evenings and well into the night praying and fasting. I went on prolonged fasts three days, seven days, ten days because I had some questions to which I wanted answers. One of my big questions was; *what was the anointing that God had given me?*

I knew my calling, and the confirming scriptures, from the early days in Mijas; Matthew 25:35-40, but without God's anointing I would be unable to fulfil my call. I knew that the anointing of God is the tangible evidence of His presence with us in our life.

As I began to go deeper into prayer the scripture that repeatedly jumped out of the bible was Isaiah 61:1..... *The Spirit of the Sovereign LORD is on me, because the LORD has anointed me to preach good news to the poor. He has sent me to bind up the broken-hearted, to proclaim freedom for the captives and release from darkness for the prisoners....*

I argued with God about this anointing because I knew it was the anointing on Jesus Christ Himself. For many nights I would argue, 'It's too much', I would say. One Sunday, as the offering basket came round, I sensed the Lord say,
'Put all your money into the offering'.
'It's all I have and it's for phone calls and postage stamps', I contested.
'Put it in', said the Lord, 'Your faith is in those coins instead of me'.
Just as I was about to drop it in to the basket, the Lord said 'count it'. I did and there was £4.17. As it went into the basket I heard the Lord say, 'I will give this back ten times'.

Later that night I was back in the college chapel arguing with God. I heard the now familiar sound of the Lord this time saying, 'Luke 4:17' so, I looked up Luke 4:17...... *The scroll of the prophet Isaiah was handed to him. Unrolling it, he found the place where it is written:* I read on to the next verse, verse eighteen..... *The Spirit of the Lord is on me, because he has anointed me to preach good news to the poor. He has sent me to proclaim freedom for the prisoners and recovery of sight for the blind, to release the oppressed....*

I couldn't argue anymore. Only the Lord knew how much money was in my pocket. There was no way I could argue my way out of that one.

Now that some of my family were saved, I set about trying to find a church for them to attend near where they lived. This meant that I was on the phone fairly regularly. One of those times my mum told me that an envelope had arrived in the post for me. How was that possible? I hadn't lived there for years, I asked her to open it. Inside was a cheque for a photo that that I had taken years ago that had recently been used in a national newspaper. It was for £45. I asked my mum to send it and the college office gave me cash for it. This was the fulfilment of God's promise to give me back ten times what I had put into the offering. I assumed that this was the money for fares home but God had other ideas.

The teaching at Bible College was phenomenal and it provided me with a strong foundation upon which I have been building ever since. I met people there who have become lifelong friends. One person I was to meet there was to become even more than that.

22

EVANGELISM

My semester was from January to April 1994 and the time was fast approaching for me to leave Lamplugh House. My fees were paid in full and I was finally ready to 'make my way north'. The money I had received from the newspaper photo was gone. God had instructed me to bless some people. I was now thinking about how I was going to get back 'home'.

One day in the college canteen I overheard a woman with a Scottish accent speaking. I eavesdropped into her conversation and she was talking about going back to Scotland for Easter. Easter was the week after college finished. She saw me tuning-in to her conversation and caught my eye. She asked if I was looking for a lift back to Scotland. We made arrangements and everything was set in place. Nancy and her young son James (his name was later changed to Israel), who was just about to celebrate his fifth birthday, picked me up from Lamplugh House. That journey was about to change my whole life. I thought that James was an amazing wee boy, happy in his skin, and I thought that his mother was an amazing woman. I fell in love with them both.

Nancy had signed-up as a day time student for a year at KF Lamplugh but we hadn't noticed each other during my time there. To our surprise we immediately got on tremendously well. At that time, Nancy was on a 'hate men campaign' having just escaped from a horrible relationship and I thought that I was only back in the UK temporarily until it was time to go back to Spain.

By the time we arrived at my parent's house in Rutherglen, Glasgow we were best friends and I invited Nancy in to meet my family. We arranged to meet each other again before Nancy had to go back down to her home in Driffield, in the Yorkshire Wolds, to complete her final semester at Bible College. We had a great time over the next week. We spent ages on the phone when we weren't with each other. When Nancy did go back we continued our late night phone calls as often as possible.

I started to attend the church which I had found for my mum, Barbara (my sister) and Peter (her husband); The Christian Fellowship Centre in Dennistoun, Glasgow. I also began working for Peter who had a coach-building business; cleaning repaired cars and delivering them back to their owners. A family in the church decided to give me their old Ford Escort car and I was able to begin visiting Nancy and James in Driffield.

I had the opportunity to baptise Peter and Barbara and Peter's secretary along with the family who gave me the car in a beautiful location in Strathaven in Lanarkshire. It was a place that I would often hitch-hike to when I was a boy and where I drove to on my red Vespa scooter. It was my 'secret place', the exact place that I had seen in my vision back in Mijas; the still, deep pool in the River Avon with overhanging trees and a high waterfall thundering into the river a little upstream.

I became the evangelist at the church. They had an evangelistic team but they had not seen any fruit from their labours for over a year. The Lord gave me a strategy that meant that no-one went out evangelising for the next few weeks. Instead we all gathered to pray and seek the way forward. It became clear that some of the team had an anointing for evangelism and others had an anointing for prayer, especially prophetic prayer.

When we did go back onto the streets, about half of the team stayed back to pray. They prayed for what was happening with the other half of the team who were out evangelising. When those who went out came back and shared what had happened with the others. Both teams were amazed that, in the Spirit, they were united. The

112

evangelists would talk about a certain situation and the intercessors would finish describing the scenario. Pretty soon around ten or twelve people each week were giving their lives to Jesus and about half of those began attending the church.

Usually, I went out with the evangelists and I found myself meeting some of the same people I used to know from the old days who were still caught up in the addiction trap and living in Homeless Units. They could hardly believe I was that person from the past and this would often trigger their own search and eventual salvation. If God could do it for me, they thought....

All was not right in that church and I began to notice it. It all came to a head shortly after I had driven the pastor around Scotland. He was looking at properties with a view to buying one as a respite home for disadvantaged children. We found a huge property, a Carnaigie Mansion near Tain and he successfully purchased it. After that, with no explanation, he told the Outreach Team to have nothing more to do with me and barred me from entering the church. I found another church to attend, along with my family members, the Kings Church in Motherwell. My mother was baptised there.

Nancy's final semester was drawing to a close and it was time to think about going to Faith Camp '94. Nancy bought a small second-hand caravan for herself, James and a friend, Nicola, who lived with them and I borrowed a small tent. I had felt, since leaving Bible College, that God was speaking to me about introducing one of the course elements into Scotland a bible reading course entitled, *The Way of the Spirit*.

The writer of the course was a Scotsman, Rev. Dr John McKay, who was the Director of Studies at Kingdom Faith Ministries. He would be holding seminars at Camp. I talked it through with Nancy and hesitantly decided to share my thoughts with John. I fully expected him to laugh at my absurd idea, after all, I was on my way back to Spain, wasn't I?

When I spoke with him he all but did a summersault for joy, 'Go and do it!' he said, rubbing his hands and laughing, 'I've been praying for years for someone to do this.' That was that. I now had the daunting task of 'doing it', but how?

23

WOTS IN SCOTLAND

Nancy returned to Scotland after Faith Camp and found a space on little farm near Strathaven where she could berth her caravan. It was August and still fairly warm in Scotland but it would be a different story in winter. For the time being, I continued to stay with my parents. We all began to attend a satellite church of the Kings in East Kilbride with Pastors Douglas and Anna Corlett. A lady at the church, Joan, kindly asked Nancy and James if they would like to move into a room in her flat in East Kilbride. They did, and I moved into the caravan in Strathaven.

As we wanted to live in Strathaven, we made arrangements for James to attend Strathaven Primary School. Once registered, it was essential that Nancy and James had a house in the school's catchments area. She looked at some options but none were right until Leigh Bent Cottage became available. It was perfect, a little semi-detached bungalow nestled into the surrounding farmland with plenty of fresh air and good walks.

We became increasingly busy establishing House Groups to study The Way of the Spirit (WOTS) course. We concentrated on building groups that were local enough for us to go to and from on the same day. As autumn progressed into winter it became too cold for me to stay in the caravan and just before Christmas 1994, John and Betty, long time friends of Nancy invited me to sleep on their sofa in their home in Darvel about nine miles south of Nancy's cottage on the same road south of Strathaven.

I remember trying to make my way quietly to bed one night after returning late from a WOTS group. As I closed the living room door, the little Santa's head hanging on the hook inside lit-up and started singing 'we wish you a merry Christmas'! Before the whole house woke up, I managed to pull it off its hook and ran through to the utility room at the back of the house where I buried it deep in a basket of dirty washing. I could still hear it, now muffled, belting out '...and a happy New Year.'

It was on the run-up to Christmas that I asked Nancy to marry me. In one of our WOTS groups in the Shawlands area of Glasgow, Fiona Merriweather gave us our first financial gift for our wedding fund.

While I was staying with John and Betty, God gave me a vision for the date of our wedding. I saw a large lake, it was very still. The water was more like oil than water. From out of the lake a monolith began to slowly emerge, it was a large gold ingot. Where the stamp of the hallmark should be there were numbers engraved. As the thick oil slowly ran off the ingot I could read 21.03.95. I knew immediately that this was to be our wedding date; the Spring Equinox, almost exactly one year after we first met.

We were now becoming increasingly more busy with *WOTS in Scotland*. We were going to have to make some serious decisions about what to do with James when we were married. We knew that we would be travelling a lot more extensively all over Scotland so, should he be placed into a residential Christian school or should we educate him at home and on the move with us? We found a good Christian school in Dumfries where we sent him for a week. He would either go to live there and attend school or we would use the curriculum they used (ACE – Accelerated Christian Education) to home school him ourselves. Nancy's mum and dad, now retired, were prepared to look after him from time to time if we needed support. For the time being, he would finish his time at Strathaven Primary School.

God had given us about three months advance notice of the wedding date and, up to that point, nothing was arranged. We needed a place for the wedding and the reception and began to look around. Nowhere seemed suitable. Pastor Douglas had a friend, La Vere Soper who had a ministry based in a castle called Crossbaskets, in High Blantyre, Lanarkshire.

We went to meet him there and asked him for the use of the castle and he agreed. From a variety of WOTS groups, people spontaneously came forward offering to help; Mike, a printer from Killin; Jean the florist from Cambuslang; Eddie the restaurateur from Gartcosh; Colin the photographer from Blantyre.... On top of all this, the Lord had whispered in my ear that Nancy and I would be going on a honeymoon!

On the morning of our wedding day, Nancy asked the Lord for a special scripture to bless her on our wedding day. Among the Scriptures that the Lord spoke to her heart there was one that stood out because it didn't seem entirely appropriate; Psalm 111:2..... *Great are the works of the LORD; they are pondered by all who delight in them.....*Hmmm.

We gave open invitations as the Lord led us and in the end 120 guests came to our wedding and reception. It was the best wedding I have ever been to! James and I danced with the other guests as we waited for Nancy to arrive. Immediately after the wedding, James came running up to me and leapt into my arms excitedly shouting 'Daddy, daddy'. I was reminded of the scripture from Psalm 2:7... *You are my Son ; today I have become your Father...* Everyone had a fantastic time. Our church had collected an offering for us to go on our honeymoon that still wasn't booked. We had tried but availability at that particular time of the year seemed to be very limited.

The day following our wedding, after prayer, Nancy and I decided to go into Glasgow City Centre, to Gordon Street, where there were a number of travel agents. We stood outside and sensed the

Lord prompt us to go into Thomas Cook. We went in and spoke with one of the sales team;

'Hi, we're Christians and we got married yesterday. The Lord said that we have to speak to you about a honeymoon'. The girl took a sharp intake of breath and said, 'God spoke to you about me?' She marvelled.

'Yes', I replied

'When would you like to go?' She asked, almost in a dream.

'As soon as possible, maybe tomorrow or the next day.' We exclaimed.

'This week has been fully booked for ages' she said, half-heartedly looking at her monitor but more interested to know how God had singled her out....

Suddenly her attention was diverted back to her screen,

'What's all this she said? Would you consider an alpine holiday?'

We had been thinking about sun, sea and sand but, in truth, we just wanted to get away.

'Where?' we asked.

'Take your pick. Apparently there's a huge thaw across Europe and all the skiers are cancelling. The tour operators are offering these cancellations at half price. French Alps, Swiss Alps, Austria...'

We looked at each other, 'Austria sounds nice'. Within ten minutes we were booked for a quality holiday in Schladming, Austria leaving in three days.

As predicted, we found that there was a thaw when we arrived. We went for a walk up a spectacular alpine gorge where the white waters of melted snow crashed their way down the mountainside. We crossed over this torrent on a little rope bridge and when we reached the rock face at the other side, there was a plaque bolted onto it. Written on it, in Austrian German, was Psalm 111 verse 2.... *Great are the works of the LORD; they are pondered by all who delight in them.....* God had brought us to where He wanted us to be. He had planned this honeymoon from the beginning.

Not long after that it began to snow until there was about twelve feet of snow lying for the rest of our time in Schladming. It was a veritable winter wonderland and we had an amazing time. One day, we took the train to Salzburg, famous as the backdrop to the iconic movie, 'The Sound of Music'. As the birth place of Mozart, Salzburg is also famous for music. It is the birth place of Mozart. The buskers to be found there were awesome. Not only were they virtuosos but they played replica instruments from the latter half of the seventeen-hundreds, the epoch of Mozart.

As the stations became more rural on our return journey back to Schladming, passengers came on and off carrying skis that they used to complete their journey to and from the train station; middle-aged women dressed in their winter woollies carried their shopping on skies instead of bicycles.

24

LOST ON A MOUNTAIN

The week after Nancy and I returned from our honeymoon in the Austrian Alps, we decided to climb a mountain on the invitation of my sister's husband Peter. Their son Darren, who was five years old, and our son Israel, who was six years old also came a long. Peter had already been on this walk to the top of Ben Venue. He said it was a 'gentle stroll'.

We parked our cars at the Loch Achray Hotel and set off to climb Ben Venue, a mountain that rises to over three thousand feet. That qualifies it as being one of Scotland's two hundred and eighty-three Munros (mountains over three thousand feet) this one towers over Loch Katrine.

It wasn't 'a dark and stormy night' and no 'shot rang out'. It was a beautiful spring day with hardly a cloud in the sky. The birds were singing and everything and everybody was just dandy.......The first thing we did wrong was at the bottom of the mountain; we ignored the red and white warning tape and the sign that hung from it. 'Closed until Easter' it read, but since this was Easter Monday we reckoned that someone had not got around to removing the tape or the sign....BIG mistake!

We all plodded on, following the footpath that would lead us to the top. So far so good, it wasn't difficult until, about one hundred feet from the summit, the weather suddenly changed and we were engulfed by a blizzard that came from nowhere. We couldn't see our hands in front of our faces. Within minutes there was a white-out and the whole mountain was covered in snow.

Since we thought we were out for a stroll we were totally unprepared; no maps, no compass, no warm clothes, nor food, on flares....nothing! The path was now hidden under the snow, so we reckoned that if we made our way to the loch-side there may be a path there that we could follow back to safety. Slipping and sliding on the slushy snow we scrambled down the mountainside until we came to a sheer drop of about five hundred feet straight into the fathomless depths of the loch. There was no path and there was no alternative. We had to climb back up the mountain to less steep terrain to look for another way back to safety.

We were all exhausted. Nancy and Barbara were distraught. They were crying and pleading for us to leave them behind. They had given up and wanted to die! I took authority and prayed powerfully in the Spirit and before I knew it, they had scaled their way back up the mountain. Clinging on to tufts of heather and using skills they did not know they had, they made it back to safer ground.

All this had taken time and Israel had developed the early stages of hyperthermia. He was disorientated and couldn't walk so, I carried him on my back. It was now dusk and we decided to split-up. Peter and his family and me and my family went our separate ways promising to send help for the others whoever found it first.

After almost nine hours on the mountain, five of them carrying Israel, we found ourselves at the foot of Loch Katrine. Like a beacon of hope, we could see a light on the other side of the loch. How could we cross over? We discovered a sluice gate over which we could cross. God was looking after us. It turned-out that the cottage with the light belonged to a mountain rescue man named, Archie. He knew exactly what to do. He stoked up his fire and put Israel in front of it. We took off his wet clothes and wrapped him in a blanket. He had 'granny skin' that was all wrinkly from being wet for so long. He soon began to thaw-out and stop shivering.

Archie could hardly believe his eyes when he saw the lights of a car back over on the other side of the loch. We said that it could be the others looking for us. He grabbed a torch and ran over to investigate.

'What are you doing up here in a car?' he hollered.

'I'm waiting for Peter' Barbara replied. Peter's with me, he's safe. Go back to the hotel and we will meet you there.'

Back at the hotel, as we climbed out of Archie's Land Rover, Barbara, in a panic-stricken voice asked,

'So where's Peter?'

'Here he is' said Archie, pointing at me.

'No! ' Barbara screamed, 'My husband Peter!!'

Archie was just about to call the mountain rescue helicopter when, puffing and panting, red-faced and ranting, Peter appeared from behind the building. He shouted at Barbara, 'Why did you turn around and go back without me? I could see the car headlights, I was almost back at the car!'

It transpired that when Peter, Barbara and Darren made it back to the hotel, Peter suggested that they should go back up the mountain in their car to look for us. They drove as far as they could over the very rough terrain and when they could go no further, Peter told Barbara to wait where she was with the car headlights on. Peter continued on foot to search for us. When Archie came with his news that everyone, including Peter, was safe, Barbara hurried back to the hotel for the rendezvous.

At last we were all safe and sound and thankful to be alive, we had some piping hot soup, compliments of the hotel. We looked back on how stupid we had been and how amazing it was that we had survived to tell this tale. Nancy and Barbara vowed that they would never climb another mountain as long as they lived.

25

VISIONS OF ANGELS

We arrived back to Scotland ready to continue as leaders of *The Way of the Spirit Bible Reading Course*. As we itinerated around churches and homes we began to criss-cross all of Scotland, sometimes travelling up to one thousand five-hundred miles in a week. We had to trust in the Lord for His provision. What started as 'faith for a fiver', for petrol to take us to our next location, soon became much more than that. We sojourned from the Outer Hebrides to the Borders and coast to coast. Almost all the time we would have James with us. He would spend his time every day doing his school work, usually with Nancy, before we set of for our next location.

John McKay had a friend, Guy Barton, who along with his sister had formed a trust to look after their family home in Kingussie, in the epicentre of Scotland. The Matthew Trust offered the use of this house to WOTS in Scotland. It was a large nine-bedroom home with three public rooms and sizeable grounds and gardens. Although it was never our home it became the WOTS base in the highlands. It was a place where we could stay when we were travelling around the highlands and a place where we could train our regional WOTS leaders for the growing work. For those who wanted to take WOTS to the next level, we could offer them the *Prophetic Bible Teachers Training Course*.

At the time when we were given the use of the house in Kingussie, a unique occurrence took place between Nancy and I while we were praying in our little cottage in Strathaven. We both entered into a vision together, the same vision. We could discuss what each of us could see and what we saw was a huge eighteen-foot warrior angel who was dressed for battle. He was wielding a massive double-handed sword above his head and slashing into the leaden sky. As he cut the clouds they receded in a speeded-up fashion leaving the sky clear and blue. At this point we heard a voice declare, 'I will give you a clear sky over Scotland'.

From that day, for the next four months, we had a cloudless blue sky over Scotland. That was a miracle in itself, but we also knew that the Lord meant He would give us an open-heaven over Scotland, a time of great favour. On the way to our house in Kingussie, as we passed through the Drumochter Pass, a fine 'Scotch mist' began to fall. As the sun backlit the mist it was as if every droplet became a prism and, in the full spectrum of the Lord's glory, God began to speak to us about the significance of multimedia, especially television, in our ministry. A day or two later standing at the window of our bedroom in Kingussie, overlooking the Spey valley, I saw the same warrior angel, still dressed for battle, but this time Nancy and I were like little children. We tumbled and rolled down the hillside. All the time this huge angel was laughing and having fun with us whilst, at the same time, vigilant and protecting.

Steadily, the number of people doing WOTS in Scotland grew to a constant two thousand. We began to have teaching days and conferences. John McKay himself came up to lead these seminars on many occasions. During one such visit to Kingussie, he saw our warrior angel for himself. John saw him standing guard at the entrance gate of the driveway leading into the house; wearing his angelic armour with his sword pointing down in the dirt with both hands on the handle holding it vertically in front of him. John was not prone to emotionalism, he really saw him.

Over the three and half years that we pioneered *The Way of the Spirit Bible reading Course into Scotland*, we met many amazing people and were overwhelmed by their generous hospitality.

We had a fellowship group of around twenty-five people, mostly involved with WOTS in the Lanarkshire area, who met regularly in our little cottage in Strathaven. We met to pray and share God's word and God certainly moved in our midst.

26

ISRAEL

In 1995, the year in which Nancy and I were married, we went back to Faith Camp. This time we took Nancy's caravan. The main speaker that year was Pastor Hector Gimenez. At that time he was the Pastor of second largest church in the world with two-hundred-and-fifty thousand members mainly in Argentina. The Pastor of the largest church was David (Paul) Yonggi Cho from South Korea. His church membership was over one million.

On our way to Camp I had collected a few stalks of wheat that had been growing at the side of the road. It was harvest time in England. At one point during the week I gave Pastor Hector our WOTS in Scotland Newsletter with a head of wheat inside. I was pleased to have made contact with him.

About one month later I was checking our phone messages by remote from a ferry on our way to Tarbert in Harris in the Outer Hebrides and there was a message from Pastor Hector's office in Argentina. They said that Hector would like to take me up on my offer and come over to Scotland. 'What!' I didn't remember inviting him to come to Scotland, but, 'hey, wouldn't it be amazing?'

I had to find a fax machine in the dusk of the evening on this remote island of Harris; an island that had not long been able to receive a television signal! I spied a building with the lights on just at the pier where the ferry came in. It turned out to be a 'workers cooperative', a community initiative, staffed by local volunteers.

The Asian GP was on duty when I went in…
'Can I send a fax from here?' I asked
'You certainly can', he replied.

'Do you have a black pen and a piece of white A4 paper?' I enquired.

He did and I began to confirm, in Spanish, that I had received the phone call and wondered how to proceed. I began to feed the hand-written paper into the fax machine but about half way in the machine began to shake and soon it was violently bouncing on the shelf. Not wanting to miss the opportunity I told the doctor that the pastor of the second largest church in the world was reading this fax, to which he loudly responded above the clatter, 'I think that God Himself is reading this fax!'

During this same time the Lord began to impress upon Nancy to change James' name. We had visited the battlefield of Culloden between Inverness and Nairn. It was there on the sixteenth of April 1746 that the Jacobite army raised by Bonnie Prince Charlie fought and were defeated in their attempt to reclaim the throne of Britain from the Hanoverians for a Stuart king.

Bonnie Prince Charlie or 'The Young Pretender' was a Jacobite. The Jacobites took their name from the Latin 'Jacobus' meaning James. For the Jacobites, King James II (of Scotland) and VII (of England) continued to reign until his death in 1701. The Jacobites denied the validity of the usurpation of the throne, at that time, by the Prince and Princess of Orange in 1688.

Jacobitism is, however, more than merely a belief that a different person has the best right to the throne. It is also a radically different understanding of the place which the monarch and the monarchy have within society. Jacobites reject the idea that the king has his authority delegated to him by Parliament. Many hold that the king's authority comes directly from Almighty God.

All of this had an impact on Nancy and I and we began to think of Jacob, the twin son with Esau born to Isaac, the son of Abraham in the Bible. The meaning of Jacob in the original Hebrew means 'deceiver or supplanter'. In the Bible, people's names are hugely important and they often are a description of the person. Not only that but every time their name is said that name is a proclamation of what it means over their life.

After an encounter with an angel of God, Jacob had his name changed to Israel. Israel means 'one who prevails with God and Prince of God'. We thought that was much better to declare than the meaning of James or Jacob, but what would our James think and what would our family think? At that time we didn't know anyone else called Israel. What would it be like growing up in Glasgow with an 'unusual' name?

We shared our thoughts with James, who at that time was having some profound encounters with God for himself. At the time he didn't say much at all. One day, as it got closer to Christmas-time, he suddenly announced from the back of the car that God was going to give him a new name for Christmas. His new name was going to be Israel. We had his name changed by deed-poll the next year, and now James is officially called Israel. After some initial raised eyebrows, his new name became accepted and most people today don't even know this story. Israel loves his name.

We have had some terrible cars in our time, one example being a Ford Sierra Estate the chassis of which had started to split. I felt sure that it was going to halve in two. The doors didn't shut properly and that, coupled with the failed heating system, meant the car was a very cold in winter. As we made our way to Kingussie from the south, we would pass through the Drumochter Pass which is four-hundred-and-sixty metres (or one-thousand-five-hundred-and-eight feet) at its highest point. In winter it was covered in snow. It was here that I first saw a whole herd of deer on the move. As I looked out on to the mountainside one gorgeous autumnal evening, I saw what I thought was heather being blown by the wind on the mountainside. On closer inspection I realised it was a herd of thousands of deer slowly moving to lower, luscious pastures.

In wintertime I could not look out of the car's side window because it would have iced-up on the inside. Nancy and I (and any unfortunate passengers) would all be wrapped up with blankets round our legs and hot water bottles on our laps as the inside of the car was literally freezing.

Around this time, John and Betty, our Best Man and Bridesmaid, bought a new car and gifted us their old one. It was a Mitsubishi Colt. We liked the idea of riding on a colt just like Jesus had done. It was an automatic car and it was a most welcome gift. However, the amount of miles we clocked up eventually took their toll and the automatic transmission began to fail. The reverse gear stopped working. This was manageable as long as we thought well ahead and parked in places from which we could drive out!

Although these car quirks are funny to relate now, at the time we understood a more meaningful, 'spiritual' message. We could not go backwards only forward. We felt that God was telling us to keep on moving forward; don't think back, don't look back and don't go back; keep going forward into victory. If I did find myself in a situation where I forgot to park facing into a space it meant that I had to ask people to give me a push backwards. This was not only humiliating but also painful!

27

THE ARGENTINIANS

The process had started for the Argentinean visit to Scotland in December 1995 and we began to pray for Pastor Hector and his team. The publicity had gone out. In one of our prayer meetings about this visit, taking place in our Strathaven cottage, the number '10,000' came into my mind, not £10,000 or $10,000 just '10,000'. It could have been ten thousand potatoes but I hoped it wasn't!

Some of the larger Glasgow-based churches began to respond positively to hosting Pastor Hector and similarly, a school, a homeless unit, a rehab centre and a prison wanted him to speak there. Our church agreed to hire a good car for us to drive him around from place to place. A contingent of Scottish leaders had agreed to meet him upon his arrival at Glasgow airport. The dates were set for Monday December 19th to Thursday 22nd December. It was the week leading up to Christmas and we knew this may have a negative affect both attendance and offerings and, what if it snowed? However, I trusted that I had heard God correctly and tried not to worry.

Everything was going to plan until the afternoon before his scheduled arrival, Sunday December 18th. Nancy, James (not yet Israel), and I were at my parents' house for Sunday dinner. My phone rang, it was a call from Pastor Hector's office in Buenos Aires. Pastor Hector was not coming! He had been invited at short notice to La Casa Rosada (the Pink House), the official seat of the executive branch of the government of Argentina and of the offices of the President, to discuss his TV programmes being broadcast on National Television. It was a tremendous opportunity and too good to miss. Nancy watched as my mouth dropped open and the colour drained from my face. I was stammering in Spanish so she couldn't understand. It was okay, they reassured me, Pastor Hector's older brother Lalo and a young evangelist also called Hector would come instead of Pastor Hector Gimenez. What was I to do?

It was too late to cancel and it was difficult to contact anyone on a Sunday. The pastors were all busy with church activities and all the offices were closed. They would never believe me, I thought. They would think it had been a set-up from the start. By the end of Sunday night I had contacted most of the key people and it was unanimously agreed that we should go ahead with everything as planned. This turned out to be the correct decision. None of us could have foreseen what was about to happen. It was to have an indelible effect on all of our lives and ministries.

Lalo came on his brother's ticket and we all met him at the airport. He was taken immediately to a church near the airport, Victory Christian Centre in Govan. Lalo began to minister to a gathering of around fifty Pastors and Leaders and I translated. Young Hector (Tito) was coming on another flight at a slightly later time, so Nancy and Pastor Anna went backwards and forwards to Glasgow airport to check on his arrival, and to look for Lalo's luggage that was still to arrive.

December is summer time in Buenos Aires. Lalo had arrived in mid-winter Scotland wearing a silk shirt with leather shoes and no socks. It became clear to the ladies that they would need to provide some winter clothes and plans were made to buy them socks, vests, sweaters and warm Parka coats.

Eventually Tito arrived and he was brought over to participate in the Govan meeting. He arrived just as the meeting was winding-up and Lalo was praying for everyone.

As soon as Nancy and Pastor Anna arrived, Lalo placed his hands on their heads and prayed for them. Like all the others he had prayed for, they went down in the Spirit and lay resting on the floor.

Pastor Anna later told us what happened. As she lay on the floor she began to feel a tremendous heat build-up in her head....'What an anointing' she thought, 'I have never felt heat like this before. Wow!' She stayed there for some time enjoying the experience, with her eyes closed, soaking it in. When she did finally open her eyes she looked up and saw that she was lying under a central heating radiator! What a laugh, so much for her super-spirituality.

28

A TASTE OF REVIVAL

The meetings went from strength to strength, breaking all previous attendance records wherever we went. Our Argentinean guests would both preach on every occasion, sharing the platform and the message but giving two distinct perspectives. Lalo was a father-figure with a Pastor's heart and Tito was a cheeky in-your-face evangelist with an endearing charm that won people over. After preaching they would invite everyone to come forward for prayer, so we ran from late to later, as the meetings progressed throughout each day. We would get home in the wee small hours of the morning after dropping the men off at their hotel, and Nancy and I would count the offerings and weep. We could see that bundles of notes, because they were scrunched-up together, had been put in from the same person and not only money was given but watches, rings, bracelets and necklaces were also put into the offering. These meetings broke all previous records for offerings given at a single meeting….and this was the week before Christmas in Scotland, a land with an overseas reputation for having a population who are so mean that they can peel and orange in their pocket to avoid having to share it with anyone!

The Argentineans told us that the revival anointing upon them was being released upon the people of Scotland, but like a boomerang they would hit their target here, and return with more force back to Argentina. The visit to Longriggend Prison was fantastic. The prison, (which is no longer used), was divided into two distinct sections. There was a young offenders (YOs) wing, where young people were kept on remand awaiting their court appearance and judgement, and there was a 'cons wing', where long sentence prisoners were located, just prior to their release, in an attempt to help them re-adjust back to a lifestyle that was more like outside.

Firstly, we visited the YO's and about twenty young men came to the meeting. They were all deathly pale and frightened but trying hard not to show it. The wardens instructed us not to attempt to lay hands on anyone and about four officers stood around the walls of the room watching. Tito began to speak and he went straight to the point;

'Look at you. You're a disgrace to your families. You have brought shame on them. You have broken your mother's hearts. But you can change that. Today you can make them proud of you. You can choose to change your life. You can turn away from your old way of life, the violence and the crime, and you can start all over again the way that God intended. Who wants to be first to give their life to Jesus?'

There was a sound of shuffling feet and downcast eyes and an embarrassing silence, then suddenly one boy stood up, then another. In rapid succession all of the boys stood, and one officer also responded. They all prayed for Jesus to forgive them and to become their Lord and Saviour from that day forward.

Next, we went to the 'cons wing' where there were only about six cells. In the first one we found a pumped-up, muscle bound, head-shaved Royal Navy sailor, who had been in the Falklands War with Argentina. Lalo told me not to translate. He went straight up to this angry young man and, in Spanish, he told him how much God loved him and how He had a plan for his life. The sailor had no idea what was being said and neither did any of the other prisoners, who were craning their necks to see what was going on. Before our eyes this hard man from Glasgow began to go as white as a sheet and his muscles began to deflate like a beach-ball with the plug pulled out. He slowly slid down the wall into a crumpled heap unable to stand up under the power of God's love. The other 'cons' watched in amazement and shouted along the passageway, 'Me next, pray for me next!'.

At the end of it all we were able to cover all our expenses and theirs and send Lalo and Tito home with $10,000 to bless the main church back in Argentina.

29

SOUTH AMERICA

In April the following year, 1996, I had an unexpected phone call,
'Hello Peter, it's Colin here.' Colin who? I thought and then I
recognised the voice. My next thought was, 'who do I know who
can impersonate Colin Urquhart?'
'I wondered how you would feel about accompanying me on a
visit to the revivals in South America?' he asked. 'We would go to
Chile first then Uruguay and then onto Argentina.' I was
flabbergasted and speechless.
'Is it to translate for you?' I asked.
'No, they will have translators. I am asking because I believe God
wants you to come with me.' He replied
'I would love to. Thank you.' I could hardly believe it. My
boyhood dream of going to South America was coming true. It was
a miracle. Paula, Pastor Colin's PA, arranged all the flights and in
May 1996 I set off for a life-changing adventure with the esteemed
Pastor and Apostle Colin Urquhart to visit the internationally
famous revivals of South America…I felt that somebody should
pinch me as it must be a dream.

When we arrived in Santiago, Chile it turned out that the translator
had been delayed and I was, therefore, called upon to translate.
There were around five thousand people gathered there for the
meeting and all was going well.

Pastor Colin has multiple variations on two basic themes which
are;
1. Who we are in Christ Jesus, and
2. If we are truly His disciples, we will hold to Jesus' teaching,
then we will know the truth and the truth will set us free.
On this occasion it was theme number 1. Pastor Colin decided to
illustrate his teaching by taking a small sheet of clean white paper

that represented the new Christian. He held this up for all to see. He then took his Bible and that represented Jesus, the Word of God. He opened the Bible and placed the clean sheet of paper inside and his point was that, as Christians, our lives are now hidden with Christ in God.

I was impacted, the profound simplicity of this revelation left me dumbstruck, which is not a good thing for a translator to be. I heard a polite cough somewhere in the distance and then a loud whisper, 'tell the people Peter'. In my moment of deep insight I had forgotten to translate for Pastor Colin. Oops!

Later after the meeting Pastor Colin shouted me over to translate something personal that he wanted to say to our host Pastor.
'Tell him God is displeased with him.' Shocked, I did as I was told. The Pastor's eyes grew wide and his mouth dropped open. 'Tell him he has been disobedient.' The Pastor's face began to grow pale. 'The Lord said that He told you to plant a church of five thousand people but instead you have been planting churches of one thousand which is easy for you.'
'It is true.' said the Pastor and he began to weep. A few months after returning to the UK we heard that the same Pastor now had a church of five thousand in the centre of Santiago. Glory to God.

As it turned out, this was the kind of translating I would be doing for Pastor Colin throughout our visit to South America. I had an incredible time. When we met Pastor Hector Gimenez in Buenos Aires, Argentina, he apologised for not coming to Scotland. In retrospect, I believe it turned out for the better that he hadn't come. Pastor Hector was so much of a big personality that people may have focussed in on him and his ministry, rather than looking to Jesus and what He was doing.

I have never met anyone who worked so hard as Pastor Hector. While we were there he spoke at his church ten times each day and he never preached the same sermon twice. He also broadcast on radio and TV every day too. The Church only closed for half an hour in twenty-four hours, usually during the night, to allow for cleaning. I remember someone asking Pastor Hector on what night they had their prayer meeting. He looked askance and said, 'We don't have prayer meetings. We pray all the time'.

Pastor Hector's church building was a former cinema in downtown Buenos Aires. The church was called, 'Ondas de Amor y Paz' (Waves of Love and Peace). The capacity was one thousand eight hundred people which meant that approximately fifteen thousand people passed through each day. They told us that it took about three days to celebrate Holy Communion. I was there with Pastor Colin for some special events to celebrate Pastor Hector's fortieth birthday. We were with well known speakers from all over the world and, in addition to what was organised at Pastor Hector's own church, there were special events organised elsewhere.

One of the places that we all went to visit was Olmos Prison just outside the city of Buenos Aires. Out of its three thousand prison population, one thousand five hundred were born again believers in Jesus Christ. The Christians occupy the whole top floor where they have painted murals depicting aspects of the life of Jesus. We had a time of fellowship with them and were introduced to the twelve pastors who look after the Christian inmates and the one Pastor who looks after them. We prayed for them and it was a blessed time. Then they asked if they could pray for us and it was awesome - these guys knew how to pray! Most of them were inside for life for heinous crimes committed when they were non-believers. Life meant for the rest of their life. Their way of escaping was to pray for the lives and ministries of the people who visited them. Olmos was once run by Satan and the Satanist Church had put an altar for sacrifices there. Now Jesus was on the throne.

The work of God started there when a Pastor was wrongly imprisoned because he had the same name as a criminal that the police were after. While the mess was being sorted out, the Christian Pastor began to pray for people and some became Christians. The Pastor went to the Governor and asked if he could hold open prayer meetings and the Governor responded by pointing to one of the worst inmates and said, 'If you can get him to become a Christian, I will allow you to have your prayer meetings.'

He was on the 'elephant floor' because that was where all the 'heavies' were. The worst, most evil of the criminals were there and the man that the Governor pointed to was the daddy of all elephants. He would go berserk and spin around with his arms out making it impossible for anyone to get near him. It would take up to six wardens to subdue him. The Pastor and his little group of Christians set their sights and targeted the elephant man in prayer. Slowly but surely, a peace began to come upon him and within a few months he became a Christian. The Governor kept his word and the prayer meetings started. Today, over half of the prison population are Christians.

That first Pastor was rightfully released but the work continued. The main Senior Pastor, at the time when we were there, was a man known on the outside as the 'Paraguayan Devil'. As a young man in prison he had learned how to make a gun. Upon his release he went to see his mother who had not visited him once while he was in prison. Her boyfriend opened the door and he shot him first and next he shot his mother. He then barricaded himself in an outbuilding with only one way in or out while he waited for the police to arrive. He shot the first two who broke the door down and then the police shot him seventeen times.

In spite of this, he did not die but he pretended to be dead. The police sent his shot-up body to the city mortuary, where it was discovered that he was still alive. They transferred him to the City Hospital and from there to the Prison Hospital. While he was there recovering another sick prisoner began to witness to him. He was a Christian and before he left the hospital, the Paraguayan Devil had given his life to Jesus and become a born again believer.

The Official 40th Birthday Celebration for Pastor Hector was held in a huge Sports arena attended by many thousands. Pastor Hector gave Pastor Colin his Rolex watch at that meeting. There was a genuine sense of joy everywhere we went in Argentina. After the rally, we sat in a restaurant overlooking the Plata del Mar to share Pastor Hector's birthday meal. Waiters served us all kinds of different meats stacked-up for selection on the blade of a sword. It was scrumptious and sumptuous.

The next day, Pastor Colin and I flew over the Plata del mar to Montevideo, Uruguay where we met a pioneer worker for Pastor Hector. José was an Evangelist doing the work of a Pastor as he planted a church in a former burlesque theatre in a seedier part of town. The whole front of the church was open on a strip where all the other open-fronts were sex shops and brothels. People were drawn into the lively Christian services taking place and, once inside, they were being touched by God and saved. José also had a radio programme that broadcast for three hours from midnight every night. I have no idea when he slept. One time when he was delivering the church offerings to Buenos Aires, travelling the long way round by road, he fell asleep. He came-to, standing beside his flattened car that had been run over by a bus full of tourists. His only injury was a little scratch on his elbow.

I sat in my hotel room thanking God on the night before we were due to return to the UK. I was counting my blessings and thanking Him for making my childhood dream come become a reality. As I had been going along, I was doing a rough tally of what this whole trip would have cost. I reckoned the total costs of flights, food, hotels and everything else all together would have been around £10,000. God is no man's debtor. The boomerang of financial blessing that we were able to send to the church in Argentina came back to us with an even bigger blessing!

30

NOOKS AND CRANNIES

Nancy and I continued to itinerate all over Scotland for three and a half years. We visited many interesting places as we travelled around the picture-postcard landscape. One such place was Glenelg, situated on the dramatic west coast of Scotland, overlooking the Isle of Skye. The world famous Glenbeag Brochs are nearby. They are some of the oldest dwellings in Scotland dating back to around 100 BC. *The drive to get there was magnificent with impossible gradients and hairpin bends. Our little WOTS group belonged to Glenelg Christian Fellowship with Pastor Donnie (who doubled as the snow-plough operator in winter), his mother Peggy and a few others. However, although the group was small, it was well worth going there for the amazing journey and the reward of feeding those hungry, isolated Christians.

Another place that was fascinating for very different reasons, was Raddery on the Black Isle. It put a shiver down our spine going there because we had to pass the Clootie Well near Munlochy on the way. Clootie wells get their name from the 'cloots', pieces of cloth, which are hung around them. They date far back into pre-Christian times and are places of pilgrimage in Celtic areas. The 'holy well' at Munlochy is said to date from AD620. The strips of cloth or rags are what is left from the clothing of sick people that have been tied to the branches of the tree as part of a healing ritual.

Our WOTS group in Raddery was hosted in the home of the Raddery School Headmaster and his wife. Raddery School was a place for Therapeutic Care, an independent residential special school for emotionally damaged young people.

The people of the area had prayed hard for a Christian to come and take up the vacant post of headmaster and Alan was their answer to prayer. He had his work cut out and he would walk around the dormitories praying for each child. There was an immense amount of spiritual activity in that place and some of Alan's stories of demonic activity were scary, to say the least. God was on Alan's side and therefore, that meant, Alan was on the winning side. One day, after being out jogging, he came in and flopped down on the sofa with the open patio windows behind him. Next thing a huge blond angel came in and straddled him, sat on his chest and prophesied to him. 'God is with you, you will overcome, you will succeed.' After that the angel left and Alan knew that it joined the angelic host that had been waiting outside before disappearing.

Although everywhere we visited had a special uniqueness that made it singular, there were some places that were distinctly exceptional and different from everywhere else. Such a place was Lewis and Harris, in the Outer Hebrides, in the North West of Scotland. There had been a revival there and I am sure that was a contributing factor. During the years 1949 to 1952, a remarkable outpouring of the Holy Spirit took place on the island of Lewis. It was so powerful that it was described as a 'visitation of God'.

Nancy and I, often accompanied by Israel, would catch the ferry from Uig on Skye for Tarbert on Harris, or from Ullapool on the mainland to Stornoway on Lewis. In Stornoway we were met by Morag McLeod from Garrabost Point. As a young girl Morag had experienced the Lewis Revival. During that time she had a vision of the horizon ablaze, where the Atlantic Ocean and the sky met. She ran to her parent's croft and, as she approached, she saw her father come out of the croft and walk to the little perimeter fence. Elated with excitement she shouted to her daddy, who ignored her, closed the gate and went back into the croft. He was a Free Church man and like many of the Free Church was not in favour of the revival.

Morag was later baptised by a visiting evangelist from Canada in a beautiful white sandy bay lapped by the turquoise blue ocean. Her parents do not know to this day why she has a photo of that place on her wall. She said if they had known they would never have spoken to her again and she would have been excommunicated from the church. When we held WOTS meetings in the villages people came secretly, but that didn't stop the Holy Spirit from moving and we had some amazing times when many were baptised in the Holy Spirit often speaking in tongues. It was very powerful.

Morag was a great host and she had the gift of hospitality. As a result, morning and afternoon, we enjoyed the delights of her home baking. I remember, when we were back on the mainland, I asked Nancy if she would like to share about what had happened when we were on the islands. She waxed lyrical about the gastronomical delights and tremendous hospitality we enjoyed there. After about ten minutes I had to interject with a polite cough and remind Nancy that we had been having WOTS meetings and it was testimony of what the Lord had been doing that I was looking for!

Some of the houses on the island were like show-houses, in fact, that is exactly what they were. From time to time when the European Sheep Subsidy came in they would pick up the phone to Argos (or somewhere similar) on the mainland and place an order for all that was in the catalogue photo of the bedroom on page eighty-nine; all that was in the catalogue photo of the living room on page one-hundred and one; and all that was in the catalogue photo of the bathroom on page one-hundred and thirty-three. They would then have it all sent to their homes on the next delivery to the island and installed and fitted as part of the store's Customer Service.

Morag would drive us to villages where our meetings were being held and, as we moved around, we would talk about the revival times. To be perfectly honest, the hungry, born again believers on the island were fed up with 'glory-chasers' who visited the island to 'see the heather on fire'. They wanted a fresh outpouring of the Holy Spirit, not a fifty years old revival revisited. We asked what it was like during those times, 'was every village caught up in the revival?'

'Not at all.' Morag responded in her soft Highland lilt, 'some villages resisted and the Holy Spirit simply went round them like a boulder in a river. Some people were too religious to see what was happening, like the Pharisees in Jesus' time, and they missed it.'

Once when we were out-and-about we went to visit Alasdair Mór ('Big' Alasdair). He was quite elderly and was sitting in a chair by the window looking out over the treeless windswept landscape of peat bogs and lagoons. A narrow tarmac road snaked its way through this bleak terrain and connected a fairly large corrugated zinc building, painted green, to the croft where Alasdair lived.

This building had been used as a church during the revival and Nancy and I had gone in there to pray before meeting Alasdair. When we were praying in the Spirit we could see people rejoicing, praising God and dancing and we shared this with Alasdair. As we did so his eyes began to well-up with tears and he looked from his window into a distance we could not see. 'Yes', he said, 'that's what it was like but the thanksgiving and praise, the rejoicing and dancing, weren't confined to that building. We spilled out onto the streets day and night, unable to contain within ourselves or any building, the great love of God that burst forth from within us.'

Another time on Harris, a WOTS meeting had been arranged in a remote cottage. The women had been busy and the baking trolley was overflowing with home-baked delights. The rain started, the wind got up and the storm grew. Our hosts stoked-up the peat fire to heat the tiny room where our meeting was to be held. The start time passed and nobody new had arrived. I didn't blame them as it was such a wild night outside.

I started the meeting for those of us who were there. I had my back to the fire facing into the room. Suddenly there was the sound of an engine outside as a minibus rolled up packed with people for the meeting. We quickly brought in more seats for the newcomers. As they filled the room I had to move closer to the fire which by now was a raging inferno. As the meeting progressed, those in attendance hung on every word and I felt that I was being braised from the back and grilled from the front. The Holy Spirit came to my rescue and there was a great release of liberty and, as the anointing worked, many were baptised in the Holy Spirit.

During our visits to the Outer Hebrides, we heard of a prophecy that had been given by a seventeenth century seer. Part of it said that 'the Isle of Lewis would be under water and the only people who would survive were those who were wearing red shoes'. In 1995 it was announced that there was going to be a new, modern ferry between Stornoway and Ullapool, that was bigger and faster, to replace the old one. We were among its first passengers. When we gathered at the pier in Stornoway to board imagine our surprise when we noticed that almost every islander who was going onboard was wearing red shoes! The name of this new ferry was the 'Isle of Lewis'.

When we visited the islands, Skye and Harris, we often stopped off at Bill and Gillian's house in Auchtertyre. It was Bill who first drove us to Glenelg and it was in their church that we heard the sermon about Jacob becoming Israel, that confirmed to Nancy, that we should change James' name to Israel. Bill and Gillian had run a large hotel in Kingussie before retiring and they knew how to look after their guests. They fed us well and I can remember sitting outside their back door, the four of us enjoying breakfast in the lovely morning sunshine. They were pivotal in the great times we had in that wider area of Wester Ross in the north-west highlands. We will never forget our visits to sub-tropical Plockton or seeing the great 'Monarch of the Glen' stags, close enough to touch, on the single-track road from Ullapool. We remember the amazing meetings in Colin's converted barn at his amazing hotel near Dornie where a Free Church minister was baptised in the Holy Spirit at a WOTS Teaching Day, and so much more. Bill and Gillian had the gift of hospitality and their influence taught us the importance of that gift for what lay ahead.

Directions to Glenelg are at the back of this book

31

MY DAD

All the while, I was still working on my relationship with my dad. When I had returned to Scotland in Easter 1994 I had stayed with my mum and dad in Mill Street, Rutherglen. Every day my dad would ask me when I was leaving. Despite this, I tried my hardest to love him. At every opportunity I would witness to him; talking, giving him Christian tracts, books and cassette tapes. I found them all in a drawer seemingly untouched.

In the February of 1996, on a Sunday afternoon, we had a family get-together at our little cottage in Strathaven. My mum and dad and her brother Jim and his wife Margaret were all there with Nancy, Israel and me. It had been a great day and the time came for our guests to go home. Outside, with the short winter days, a frost had fallen and it was slippery underfoot. Going down the two steps of our front door, my mother slipped and almost fell. For some illogical reason, instead of being compassionate, I was angry at her and roughly bundled her into our car and took her home.

I dumped my mum and dad and went to our monthly regional churches gathering at the Kings in Motherwell. The meeting had started and I immediately joined in with the worship. With my hands raised and eyes closed, I heard a voice ask me, 'What are you doing here? Get down that road and apologise to your mother!' I told Nancy I was going out but I would be back.

I went into my mum and dad's house and went straight to where my mum was sitting watching TV in the living room, I sat on a stool in front of her and I asked her to forgive me. I began to cry and she comforted me. I was so sorry and explained how wrongly I had behaved as a son and as a Christian. My dad, who was sitting in another chair beside my mum said, 'Are you listening Barbara?'

Both my mum and I, surprised at his interjection, turned to look at him and I just knew in my spirit that my dad was ready to ask Jesus into his life.

'Have you been listening to those tapes I gave you?' I asked

'What if I have?' he retorted.

'Are you ready to get saved?'

'I am' he said, and right there and then, I led my father in prayer to his salvation in Christ Jesus.

In September that same year (1996), Nancy and I received a phone call while I was ministering in Stoke-on-Trent informing me that my dad had had a massive stroke. We rushed back to Scotland and went straight to the Victoria Hospital in Glasgow. The prognosis was bad and we were told that my dad would never walk or talk again and, if he did recover, he would be like a vegetable. I knew that I had to pray for a miracle but I also knew that my mum and my sister, who were also there, would need to make up their minds whose report they would believe. Did they have the faith to believe that God could, and would, heal my dad? Barbara said she could not believe and left my mum, Nancy and I to pray.

I also felt that I should anoint my dad with oil in accordance to what the bible says in James 5:14-15..... *Is any one of you sick? He should call the elders of the church to pray over him and anoint him with oil in the name of the Lord. And the prayer offered in faith will make the sick person well; the Lord will raise him up....* I poured almost a bottle of olive oil over my dad's head and prayed. Throughout this, with his un-paralysed arm, he kept reaching out in front of him, trying to catch something that we could not see. I thought that he maybe thought that there was one of those triangles suspended above his bed with which he could pull himself up.

In less than one week my dad was attempting to get out of bed and he could talk. Among other things, I wanted to know what this 'reaching out for something' was all about. My dad explained that when he was having the stroke it was like he was caught-up in a whirlwind and he felt that he was falling backwards into darkness. A figure appeared to him silhouetted against a brilliant light and began to call his name, 'Alex…..Alex….' over and over. My dad reached out to take hold of the figure's outstretched hand and he said that he had never felt a grip like it. It would not let him go. 'Who do you think it was?' I asked. 'It was Jesus, of course' my dad replied.

By Christmas time my dad was able to walk and the hospital allowed him home for a few days. We danced and took photos to show to the hospital staff who said he would never walk again. He lived for another six years after his stroke. Six years that he would not have had if he hadn't met Jesus in the whirlwind. He went home to be with the Lord in 2002 at the age of sixty-seven.

My dad grew up as hard man in the gangs of Glasgow's East End, the 'No Mean City' of the 1950's. His Father died when he was still a toddler and he was raised by his mum and his older sisters. He was an angry, violent man. His knowledge of the world was simple and basic. He lived on his primeval instincts for survival. In order to survive in his world, he had to know which areas were safe in the close boundaries of his home.

Once my schoolboy friend George and I talked my dad into coming hill walking with us. We decided to take him up to the top of Ben Lomond. It is an easy mountain to climb but it rises to over three thousand feet and from its summit the views are magnificent. We all plodded upwards and onwards for about six hours until we reached the top. It was a glorious day of cloudless blue skies.

We could see Loch Lomond's eighteen miles of glistening splendour and the surrounding mountains spreading northwards to the Grampians and the Highlands beyond. To the south we could see the Southern Uplands and to the east the North Sea and to the west the Atlantic. What an awesome view. When I turned to see my dad's reaction, he was already was half way back down the mountain. The panoramic vista from the top had blown his mind and he couldn't take it in. He had stepped outside of the safety zone of self preservation and was confronted with the overwhelming reality of a world beyond his control.

32

DRUMCHAPEL

The demand for our WOTS Teaching days began to grow and although Rev. Dr John McKay led many of them, he could not lead them all. Other speakers, including Colin Urquhart from Kingdom Faith Ministries came to lead. I remember on one occasion Jarrod Cooper was our speaker. He had been the worship leader at KF Lamplugh when Nancy and I were students there and he later became internationally known for writing 'King of Kings, Majesty'.

The first time Jarrod was with us was when the charismatic manifestations of the Holy Spirit, that we had first seen from the Airport Church in Toronto, Canada, were at their most extreme. On the morning of the Teaching Day Jarrod was so 'drunk in the Spirit' that he could hardly stand. His speech was slurred and he was incoherent. What were we going to do? We expected over one hundred people from a wide area of Scotland to turn up expecting to be fed from God's word. Jarrod (and to our relief, God) assured us that everything was going to be alright. Sure enough, we did have a pretty unorthodox meeting but as Jarrod prophesied to many of the people there, with words of knowledge and words of wisdom he impacted and permanently changed the lives of the people to whom he spoke.

WOTS was never meant to be a para-church or a substitute for attending a recognised church where a pastor would get to know his congregation. It was a course written with the express purpose of raising-up true disciples of Jesus and these, in turn, would raise up more disciples. Nancy and I learned so much from coordinating and actually doing the course and that experience provided us with the bedrock foundation for what we are doing today. Three of the key words that run through the whole course, and potentially provide the answers to most of the questions, are; *faith, obedience* and *sacrifice*. In fact these three words summarise the life of Jesus Christ and, as such, they also express the expected lifestyle of every Christian follower (disciple) of Jesus Christ.

We had tremendous times, saw amazing places, witnessed some awesome miracles, met fantastic people and helped to nurture and help many of them. Through WOTS we were able to show people how to live out their lives, led by the Holy Spirit, as true disciples of Jesus. However, after three-and-a-half years, it was time for a change and Nancy and I began to cry out to the Lord to give us an opportunity to get among the non-saved; among people who didn't know Jesus.

It didn't take long for God to answer our prayers. On our way to a leaders meeting at Kingdom Faith in Roffey Place, our flight was cancelled due to bad weather. It was January 1997. Rather than go straight home we stopped in at the Victory Church in Govan. Alex Gillies, the Pastor, was there and we sat in the church café to chat for a while. Alex was thinking about getting married and he asked us how a person knew when they were in love. We laughed and chatted some more. Alex asked us how our ministry was going and we explained what we were praying for. Immediately, Alex asked us if we wanted an empty church building. He had just been given one in the place where he had grown up and first ministered in Drumchapel, Glasgow. We were interested and arranged to meet him and Arthur, his assistant Pastor, at Drumchapel the next day. We met and prayed and agreed to take on the building until Easter.

We put the word around and began to plan for our first church service in The Victory Church, Drumchapel. Many of our WOTS workers from the Glasgow area were keen to join us for our first Sunday but the devil wasn't happy. Right from the start local youths began to petrol-bomb the building and trash any cars that were parked there. Sometimes they would steal our cars, drive them to the local woods and burn them out. It wasn't easy.

This went on for weeks. Once as I was leaving the building, I narrowly dodged a brick that was thrown. I heard the taunt being carried in the wind; 'We are the Romans you are the Christians....' (sick Glasgow humour!). Unperturbed, we continued to pray and to meet. We started a Bible College and many of our WOTS people attended. One night we were praying at the front door of the church building and I could see some figures moving around in the shadows and in the bushes outside. We continued to pray and a few missiles were thrown in our direction. The next night it was the same but this time the figures, wearing masks came out of the shadows but still continued to goad us. On the third night they came up to the door and asked us what we were doing. 'We're praying for you'. They responded with a few profanities. 'What do you do in there anyway?' they asked. 'It's a church, do you want to come in?'

With bravado and a swagger they came in and sat around. There weren't many of us there, it was a Tuesday and no meetings were scheduled. We started to talk to them in an unthreatening, friendly way. They relaxed, four boys in their mid teens. Before the end of the night all four of them had given their lives to Jesus. It was a miracle and a sovereign work of God's grace.

Not long after that things began to change for the better. It was as if there had been a by-election in the heavenlies and Jesus had been voted in.....

33

BREAKTHROUGH

Our little worship team was made up of Nancy on keyboards, Evert on guitar and a local boy we were teaching to play drums. Evert was a Kingdom Faith (KF) Roffey graduate who was Dutch but had lived in Glasgow before and had returned to Glasgow after going to Roffey. He was an IT genius and he lived in the basement of our church.

I would rise early every morning and seek God for the Prophetic Bible Teaching message for our Bible College that day. I would record what I was going to teach onto a personal Dictaphone. When I came into our church building I would give the tape to Evert who would transcribe it and give me the typed transcription immediately after our morning prayers and devotional time. These were my teaching notes for that morning. We did this every day when I had classes in our Bible College. Evert is still my friend and will remain so. He now lives in Holland and Nancy and I had the honour of being guests at his wedding in July 2007 when he married a beautiful Dutch girl called Mieke.

As they were playing one Sunday at church, the worship team looked at each other in a most peculiar way. Each was convinced that the others had been secretly practicing because they sounded so good. The worship was amazing and, as we continued, it became clear that it was not our musicians who had dramatically improved, it was the angels who accompanied them that brought in a brand new, never-heard-before dimension to the music. During the worship, the sanctuary door burst open and in rushed a flush-faced plump woman in her mid thirties with a gaggle of five children around her saying, 'I had to come, I had to come! It was the light in the sky. I saw it from miles away and jumped on a bus to follow it. It's there above the roof, I had to come.' We went out to look but the light that had led her to us had gone, job done. We explained that there had been angels worshipping with us that evening and she understood that God had brought her to our church to meet Jesus. She gave her life to Jesus and a sublime peace came upon her. I'm not sure if she got the No. 9 bus back home that night or simply floated home on cloud nine!

Soon, more and more people started to get saved from the local community. Drumchapel has the stigma of being a dysfunctional inner city housing estate, or 'scheme', full of undesirable people that nobody wanted as neighbours. People were dumped there from all over the city of Glasgow. These included long term unemployed and unemployable with addiction problems and criminal records. Most had little or no education which meant that our classical model of Bible College was not going to work and, therefore, I had to rethink my strategy.

God gave me a strategy, an holistic curriculum that focused on five key elements of Christian discipleship; physical, practical, spiritual, creative and ministerial. It would be called 'Training for Life' (TFL). I made a collection of videos and put seven of them together in a series called 'Foundations'.
These covered the preliminary steps of foundational Christian teaching….

Teaching 1 - Brings the assurance of our salvation
Teaching 2 - Sees us baptised in the Holy Spirit
Teaching 3 - Releases us in the gifts of the Holy Spirit
Teaching 4 - Shows us how to get closer to Jesus
Teaching 5 - Reveals our new identity in Christ
Teaching 6 - Brings the gift of discernment to guard against deception
Teaching 7 - Sends us out in the light

I started to build a library of resources for the curriculum. It was made up of teaching notes, audiocassettes and books. However, it became clear that in order to give the new Christians from Drumchapel a fighting chance, we would need to find a residential place for them to participate in our TFL course. Nancy and I began to look around for a suitable building. During this time we felt that the Lord was encouraging us to 'give away what you have and I will give you what you need'. What we had was the use of a large house in Kingussie. What we needed was a large house closer to Glasgow, maybe about an hour's distance from the church. Far enough away to feel removed from 'familiar' Drumchapel. We thought a place with about twenty rooms would be more than ample. A small hotel, for example, with all the residential specifications (health and safety, etc..) already in place.

I shared the vision with our Bible College students and mid-sentence the Lord stopped me and rebuked me.
'Your vision is too small. It's not twenty rooms, it is seventy rooms.'
I gulped and shared with the students what the Lord had just told me. We all gulped and I set about writing down the vision to share it with our supporters.

Unfortunately, up to this point, everywhere we looked at either had the lead stolen from the roof or had been badly vandalised and would cost hundreds of thousands of pounds to repair. We had in mind to give Ardselma, the house in Kingussie, to a young family who had been part of our very first WOTS group almost four years before. Andy and Carla had been so impacted by WOTS that they had given up their rented council house in a run-down area of Coatbridge, Lanarkshire and, together with their two young daughters, had gone to KF Bible College in Roffey Place.

After two years when they completed the course, they had no home to return to, so Nancy and I invited them to come and live at

Ardselma, Kingussie. Carla was pregnant. Now that Nancy and I were going to be based in the Glasgow area, Kingussie was too far away for us. After much discussion and prayer we passed the reigns for WOTS in Scotland to Andy and Carla. At the same time we put a fleece before the Lord saying that if he really wanted us to run with the church in Drumchapel then He would get us a house nearer the Church. We were still living in our little cottage in Strathaven and that, at peak times, was a two hours commute to Drumchapel.

Within days, a person turned up at our church who, it transpired, had a sister who lived in a rented farm just over the hill, out of sight from our cottage. Anne and her husband John had a house in Torrance that they were very keen to let out to raise the rent money for the farm. We met up and went to see their house in Torrance. It was ideal for our needs and an arrangement was made. Within a few quick weeks we moved into our new home in Torrance which was only seven miles, or fifteen minutes commute, to the church in Drumchapel. The Lord had responded to our fleece and we knew that it was right for us to continue with the work in Drumchapel.

34

KILCREGGAN HOUSE

When John, whose house we were renting in Torrance, heard that we were looking for a large property an hour from the church in Drumchapel he asked us if we had ever been to see Kilcreggan House. We had never heard of Kilcreggan, never mind Kilcreggan House.

As it happened, around this same time, we decided to trade in our old car for a better one and as part of the incentive for the trade-in the garage offered us a second car along with the Vauxhall Carlton we wanted. It was a little Fiat Panda. It was in this little Fiat car that we set off to find Kilcreggan House.

As we drove up the sweeping driveway and saw the massive mansion our hearts leapt within us and we knew that this was the place that the Lord wanted us to have. We had arranged to look around inside. The house had been empty for about four years and was a little stuffy but, despite this, and the fact that the decor was locked in a 1970's time-warp, we both fell head-over-heels in love with the place. 'Kilcreggan House' also came bundled with a whole assortment of cabins and out-buildings and spanned over three acres of land.

Lynne, one of our ministry intercessors had been praying for us to find the right ministry base but she wasn't simply praying for a big empty building. She knew that we would need things like bedding, crockery, cutlery, furniture, etc.... Kilcreggan House was like the *Marie Celeste*. It was as if the previous occupants WEC (World Evangelisation for Christ) had been spirited away and everything that they had been using was left behind for us to use.

How were we going to be able to afford to buy Kilcreggan House? We had no money to speak of, but one thing we knew for certain, was that if the Lord wanted us to have it, He would make it possible for us to buy it. We left after a few hours of looking around and a plan slowly began to formulate itself within us. We approached WEC and asked them if they would allow us to visit Kilcreggan House to pray once a week to confirm and reassure us that the Lord really did want us to buy the house. They agreed. Over the next six months our 'one day a week' grew into almost every day. We would take groups of people down with us and we would prayerfully seek God for direction. We compiled a dossier as thick as a telephone directory that was full of scriptures and prophetic words that the Lord impressed upon us. It was an awesome time.

Jan, a friend of ours from The Wirral near Liverpool, came up to visit us and to pray with us around this time. She said to us one day, 'the Lord was very specific when He told you that the place He has for you has seventy rooms. Why don't you count the rooms that are here?' We set about counting all the bedrooms, sitting rooms and lounges. When we came to the back row of cabins we counted, sixty-eight, sixty-nine....seventy! God was confirming that we were in the right place.

During these six months the Lord also instructed us to create a charity that He told us to name, *The Way Christian Ministries*. The name made perfect sense to us; Jesus is the Way, our surname is Stanway, the early church were called 'followers of the Way' and, for around four years, we had been itinerating with a bible reading course called The Way of the Spirit. We worked with the same solicitors used by Kingdom Faith Ministries and eventually our charity was formed and registered, in 1997, as a recognised Scottish Charity number SCO 27189.

There was now a queue at the door of recently saved young men from Drumchapel waiting for somewhere to go to start our TFL course. We didn't have the money to buy Kilcreggan House but when we spoke to WEC they agreed to let us rent for one year at the cost of £1,000 per month. If we still couldn't afford to buy after that they would put it back on the market for sale.

Immediately, we filled the house with trainees and volunteers. We had a full timetable of daily activities from early morning until evening in all five key areas of our curriculum. We had a core of around twenty-five residential trainees with people leaving and joining on a regular basis, such was the instability of the lifestyle of the people in our church. We also had a marvellous and growing group of volunteers.

Meanwhile the work at Drumchapel continued to grow and develop. I, personally, was going through the ordination process with the Assemblies of God although, the church itself, was looking and behaving less and less like a traditional (AOG) church. I was splitting my time between Kilcreggan House, working to establish the new Training for Life Centre, and the work at Drumchapel. As people heard that Kilcreggan House was up-and-running again, we began being asked to host conferences for other churches and to take groups of foreign students on mission to Scotland. As part of their activities we would take foreign students into Drumchapel and that was invariably an eye-opening, even eye-popping, experience.

I remember once taking a group of American students into Drumchapel and afterwards over-hearing them talk in our mini-bus on the way back to Kilcreggan.
'Did you hear those children? Every one of them spoke in tongues!' they exclaimed.
I could hardly refrain from laughing out loud. Although there were some tongues talkers among our children, what these students had

heard was the incomprehensible babble of a broad Glaswegian accent!

When we facilitated conferences for other church groups and Christian organisations our trainees and our trainee volunteers were very much involved. They would help prepare the house for the group coming and clean up afterwards. While our guests were with us our trainees and team would be involved in serving the food and washing up. This was how we generated funds to pay the rent and the bills. It was great 'life training' for our 'unemployable fifth-generation of unemployed', those 'lay-about drug addicts and alcoholics'. The Lord had taught me back in Mijas, *'If a man will not work, he shall not eat'* (2 Thessalonians 3:10).

Most of the hospitality work took place at the weekends, including Friday set-up and Monday strip-down. Wednesday was normally our day off. Tuesdays and Thursdays were days for practical maintenance around the house and every morning we all gathered together to start the day with a devotional time and prayers. We didn't host guest's conferences every weekend. Therefore, when we could, we would sometimes hold our own conferences, with visiting speakers. I would teach up to eighteen hours throughout the week. Some of our most stimulating curriculum conferences were our creative ones. They were times of prophetic worship, prophetic painting, poetry and creative writing. Invariably, the Lord would give us the tune and words for a new song in which we would all have collaborated.

Sometimes we would take our trainees over to northern France to a place called Thumeries. The nearest city was Lille and we would have evangelistic outreaches there and in other towns. In Thumeries there is an authentic château with a moat and a draw bridge. It is called Château Blanc and it dates back to 1541. We would work there on renovation projects. Château Blanc is the

French base for the missionary organisation called World Horizons.

Not too far from Thumeries is a place called Vimy Ridge. At Vimy Ridge more than two hundred thousand soldiers were killed and wounded in only four days of fighting, in April 1917, during the First World War. We would take our trainees there to see for themselves the huge cost that had been paid by our grandfathers and great-grandfathers who won for us the freedom that we enjoy today. The Bible commands us to 'remember the days of old' (Deuteronomy 32:7).

35

HEPATITIS C

During the year of renting, God introduced us to people who would be instrumental in acquiring and maintaining Kilcreggan House. Bobby, a business entrepreneur, showed us how to put a business plan together and the best way to borrow money from the banks. We met a Christian solicitor and a Christian Business Banking Manager. We devised a *'Buy-a-Brick'* campaign to help raise the money for our deposit and donations started to come in. They ranged from a couple of pounds to, on occasion, a couple of thousand pounds.

Around the same time, court proceedings were started against us. This was to take Nancy and I through a traumatic year of legal wrangling over a very personal custody matter that was ultimately to put our faith in the dock. To our shock and horror two of the witnesses against us were close family members who claimed to be Christians. They stood in court, on oath, not only slating us, our capability as parents and the work we were doing, but they also mocked and ridiculed The Pentecostal Church and the work of the Holy Spirit and sneered at the gift of tongues. We had some close friends and family members who stood up for us in the court to our defence. There were others who supported us in prayer, including some intercessors that even came to sit at the back of the court to pray quietly.

Our year of renting was coming to an end and although we had managed to have the asking price reduced by £100,000, we were still short of the £50,000 that we needed for the deposit. A friend of my grandmother, Betty, had indicated that she would like to help us. We arranged a suitable time and Nancy and I went to see her at her home in Gourock. She agreed to give us a loan of £20,000, in fact she wanted to gift us the money. However, as she wasn't part of TheWayCM and we didn't really know each other, I had an official loan agreement drawn-up by our solicitor with the understanding that we would pay it back at £1,000 per month.

We submitted our business plan, through our new Christian Business Banking Manager, and the bank agreed to give us a loan for the remainder of the money to buy Kilcreggan House over the next ten years. The day that we signed the loan agreement with the bank coincided with the same precise day that we heard of the court's decision to grant Nancy and I exclusive custody for Israel; a triumphant outcome to a horrendous year in court. It was October 1999.

A few weeks after the loan papers were signed, Betty from Gourock suddenly died. Betty had never married, had no children and her niece Josephine, was her executor and beneficiary. When she discovered the agreement between her Auntie Betty and ourselves, she thought that we had duped her auntie out of £20,000. She demanded immediate repayment. We didn't have the money to do that but we did have a legal document signed by her auntie. With our solicitors help, we came to a new agreement to repay Betty's loan at £2,000 per month which, along with the bank loan repayments and the on-going overheads, was a real challenge to our faith, but by the grace of God we managed it.

While living in Strathaven, an on-going year-long investigation into some personal health problems had led to the discovery that I had diabetes. My liver function tests indicated that I was a chronic alcoholic or drug user.
'Not any more', I said to the doctor. 'I'm a minister now and have not touched alcohol since 1993'.
'Let's do some more tests,' he said.
These tests led to the discovery that I had the Hepatitis C virus and the genotype was 1, the worst kind. It is sometimes called, 'the silent killer'. Apparently 'non A - non B Hepatitis' had now been

renamed and was called Hepatitis C. The Hepatitis virus I had contracted about fifteen years earlier had not 'gone away', as I was told. It had stayed in my blood stream and during all that time had been working away at destroying my liver.

The doctor sent me along to a clinic at Ruchill Hospital, now closed, where I spoke with a specialist about a possible treatment using interferon and ribavirin. These were the early days of this kind of mild chemo-therapy treatment and it involved weekly injections for fifty-two weeks. As I sat in the dilapidated grounds of that run-down hospital, listening to active drug addicts talk the nonsense that comes with heavy drug use, I decided, in the balance, that I wasn't so ill and would forego the treatment.

During the time that we lived in Torrance I had never visited a doctor. However, when we moved to live in Kilcreggan, one of the requirements for registering with the local GP was to undergo a comprehensive medical examination. In early November 1999 my doctor sent me along to speak with Dr Mills, the top liver specialist consultant at Gartnavel General Hospital in Glasgow. He told me that there was cirrhosis of my liver and that this could lead to the need for a liver transplant.
'When?' I asked,' In ten years or so?'
'Maybe sooner than that.' He replied.
'Five years?'
'Mmmm.'
'Two?' I asked
'Within the next year' he said.
I was flabbergasted, a liver transplant! I didn't even feel particularly ill.

Towards Christmas time in 1999, on the way to our children's Christmas party at the church in Drumchapel, I was suddenly floored by a pain unlike anything I had ever experienced. I was doubled-up with excruciating pain in my abdomen. Nancy, who by now did most of the driving, pulled into a clinic in Dumbarton that we passed on our way to Drumchapel and a doctor came out to examine me. I was still writhing around on the floor of our minibus. He made arrangements for me to be admitted immediately to the local hospital, the Vale of Leven. As Nancy rushed me over there I passed-out in the back of the van.

At the hospital they discovered that I had haemorrhaged from my liver and, when they looked at my case notes, they discovered why. They contacted Dr Mills and Sister Spence, Dr Mill's assistant, and they moved quickly to make arrangements to have me sent to the Royal Infirmary in Edinburgh in order to go through the assessment process for a liver transplant. I was allowed home to Kilcreggan House briefly to be with my family for Christmas and New Year.

I was ill and no-one was in the mood to head up to the city centre of Glasgow or to jostle with the crowds to enter into the revelries for the 2000 Millennium Celebrations. We decided instead to head to the church of our friend Bill Mercer in St Catherines in Argyll.

We took a mini-bus load of boys, trainees from the house, and set off for what turned out to be a lovely time. They had a guest speaker, who was unknown to me, who had a prophetic ministry. At one point during the proceedings he singled me out and looked straight at me, 'Someone is going to have to die so that you can live.' He prophesied. Nancy and I spiritualised this to mean that he was talking about Jesus who died for us on the cross at Calvary so that, by believing in Him, we can live for ever. Of-course, in hindsight, we now know that he was talking about the liver donor who would have to die for me to have his/her liver in order for me not to die.

At the beginning of January I was re-admitted to the Vale of Leven Hospital and transferred to The Scottish Liver Transplant Unit

(SLTU) at the old Royal Infirmary in Edinburgh. This is the only hospital that does liver transplants in Scotland. I spent most of the next two months in the hospital leading up to my assessment.

Our volunteers, and Nancy's mum and dad, were excellent and they did their best to hold everything together. Nancy, who wanted to be by my side, had to make the journey back to Kilcreggan to stay for a few nights every week.

Rev. Hugh Black, the founder of the Struthers Memorial Churches and a well respected man of God, prolific author and Apostle in Scotland, would phone me most days and make the journey down to Kilcreggan once a week to teach the boys. We also had some of our friends come to Kilcreggan House to have an input into our trainees lives. Among them were, Rev. Dr John McKay, Rauna May, (an international speaker and Pastor from Vancouver, Canada) and Judith Butler; an intercessor and teacher on prayer, (who had been taught by Gordana Toplak), from Kingdom Faith Ministries.

I was also allowed home from time to time but I was becoming more and more ill. My skin was now yellow like a banana. The toxins in my blood, that are normally filtered out by the liver, were now circulating through my brain making me confused and very tired. I went on a mission to northern France at this time but hardly remember anything about it. We decided to go on the Hovercraft. However, I can remember that the operators switched us to the Sea Cat at the last minute but on the way back it was onboard the Hovercraft.

The sail is referred to as a flight and the crew as flight attendants. All the terminology is similar to that used when you fly. I found my seat, buckled up and fell asleep. Apparently there was a huge storm on the English Channel that caused outrageous turbulence. Everyone on board was sick - everyone, that is, except me. I slept undisturbed the whole way. It was very fool-hardy of me to go in the first place and it was only the divine protection of God that kept me alive on that mission.

By now many of our friends had become aware of my condition and prayer began to circulate on my behalf. This intercession was to grow to a world-wide phenomenon with many, many thousands of people praying for me continually all round the world. Key leaders also began to open their large attendance meetings in prayer for me.

While I was in hospital for my assessment, I received a few visitors, among whom was Father Lawrence. He said that he was a Roman Catholic missionary who had been in Brazil for many years. I do not know how he knew about me, but apparently on his way to take a meeting about the Holy Spirit in Stirling, he felt led to come and ask me to pray with him.

I was in a public visitors' room when he came in. The other visitors felt the need to leave him alone with Nancy and me. He went down on his knees, in the middle of the floor, and asked me to lay my hands on him and pray for him to have a fresh infilling of the Holy Spirit. He got to his feet rejoicing and thanking God. After my transplant he came back to see me while I was recovering in the High Dependency Unit. Again he wanted me to pray and lay hands on him. However, as I was too weak to lift my arm, unperturbed, he lifted my hand and plopped it on his head. I said a simple prayer and he left, smiling from ear to ear. Did all that really happen? Nancy was with me and she saw it but it felt quite surreal.

During the assessment Nancy and I met with the team of twenty people who would be involved in my transplant. This enabled us to ask questions, which they welcomed, and for them to inform us with very accurate information regarding the transplant. This information provided our growing army of intercessors with precise prayer targets and miracles began to happen. By now the transplant team, patients, visitors and ourselves could all clearly see that Almighty God was in control.

At one stage it was discovered that the Portal vein, which is one of the two main sources of blood supply to the liver, was blocked. Nancy saw this on the scan monitor. The Portal vein, about the diameter of a thumb, was narrowed like an egg-timer and only little spurts of blood were getting through. However, more information was needed and another scan was scheduled. We told people of the findings and the next scan showed no blockage! What it did show was that the other blood supply, that came through a series of arteries, was blocked. There was talk of grafting-in other arteries from different parts of my body or even using artificial arteries. Plans were made to do this extra surgery at the time of the transplant.

Jesse Duplantis, a well-known preacher from the USA, came to hold an event in Meadowbank Sports Arena near Edinburgh. Nancy had become friendly with the host Pastors, whose church she had been attending on Sundays, when she was staying in the relatives' room at the hospital. She arranged for me to be invited to the event and sit in the front row for Jesse to pray for me at an appropriate time during the meeting. He knew about my situation and he knew where I was sitting.

He began to talk about a man who was there with liver failure. He went on to describe accurately all that was wrong with me. All of our friends who had come along to Jesse's meeting were very impressed because they thought that Jesse was operating in the Spiritual gift called the 'word of knowledge' and that God Himself had given Jesse accurate 'inside' information. We still laugh about that yet. Jesse called me forward and prayed with me to the accompaniment and cacophony of one thousand five hundred fervent intercessors. I did feel an improvement after Jesse prayed but continued as a patient in the hospital.

36

LIVER TRANSPLANT

The assessment itself took two weeks. After the assessment it was agreed that I should have a liver transplant.

'How long does Peter have to live?' asked Nancy.

'A maximum of two months' they replied. In her heart Nancy knew, in reality, it was less than that.

'How long does it take to find a matching liver?' She enquired.

'It can take up to a year.'

I was duly released from the hospital on Friday 24th March, 2000, after the transplant coordinators had spoken with me, and activated my name on the transplant list. They would contact me when a suitable liver was found.

On the following Sunday I felt good enough to preach in the church (don't ask me what I talked about!) and late that night, the phone rang to inform us that a matching donor liver had been located and that an ambulance would arrive in half-an-hour to take us to the SLTU. Blue lights and sirens hastened the way to Edinburgh but the journey still took about two hours. However, after consultation among the transplant team, it was decided that the donor liver was not good enough and I was sent back home. All the way through on that journey in the ambulance, Nancy was silently shouting, 'No!' to God. She believed that God would perform a supernatural miracle to give me a new liver without surgery. Now, in hindsight, we know that He had been telling us that I was going to have a transplant. The signs had been there as far back as the time in the little church in St Catherines for the Millennium. Yet God would not move until Nancy gave Him permission.

As my kidneys began to close down my body filled up with fluid. I was taking the maximum amount of diuretics to reduce the fluid. I remember, one night, lying on the sofa at home and staring incredulously at my foot. It looked like an inflated rubber glove. Nancy thought it was hilarious and couldn't stop laughing, probably because of nerves, I couldn't stop crying because I knew I was dying. As death approaches, the dying person's circulatory system will begin to shut down. My liver had stopped working and now my kidneys were shutting down.

For a few days at the house crows had begun to bang on the windows. It intensified as the days went on and their knocking turned into violent thrashing so much so that we could see their saliva smeared all over the windows. If we chased them away they simply came back to another window. It became so bad that we contacted the RSPB (The Royal Society for the Protection of Birds) to ask them what was going on. They explained that crows were territorial birds and, when they saw their reflection in our windows, they thought that it was another bird in their territory, therefore, they flew at their own reflection to attack it and chase 'the intruder' away. They said if we put the silhouette of an eagle in our windows, the crows would think it was a bigger bird and not attack it. We tried it and it seemed to work but the Lord was soon to reveal to us what was really happening…..

Just before Mr Black arrived for his usual Thursday night teaching session, Nancy relented and decided in her heart that if it had to be a transplant that would save my life, then so be it. She went to Mr Black to ask him if he had a 'word from God for her' concerning my condition. 'Nancy, you know that I do not give 'words' unless I have clearly heard from God.' He said. As he began to teach Nancy had a vision of Mr. Black calling me forward for prayer and me falling to my knees at his feet. A few minutes later what Nancy saw in her vision actually happened. To her shock, Mr Black's prayer was brief and to the point. All he said was, 'Lord, whatever you are going to do, do it swiftly.'

That night Nancy felt that I was going to die. She lay awake watching my shallow breathing that would stop altogether from time to time. She went to the toilet at 5.45 a.m. and said to the Lord, 'Do whatever is necessary but don't let Peter die.' At 6.00 a.m. the pager went and we phoned the hospital. An ambulance was on its way to take us through to Edinburgh.

Twelve long days had passed and I was back at the SLTU and, this time, the donor liver was good; the transplant would go ahead. We met with a new person, K.K. Madhavan, the surgeon who would perform my transplant. The surgeon scheduled for me had already done another transplant throughout the night and KK was now 'familiarising himself' with my case notes! What was this last-minute switch? Later I was to find out….

Prepped and ready, I drifted into a place as near death as its possible to go without actually dying. After a ten hour operation, I was hooked-up to life support equipment in the intensive care ward where God gently allowed me to 'bleep and whirr' my way towards some kind of stability. I began to make a strong recovery. A few days after the operation I enquired about the extra arterial grafting that was scheduled. I was informed that once inside my body it was discovered that there was no blockage whatsoever.

By now even the most ardent unbeliever was acknowledging that God was very much involved with my welfare. Around that time I also discovered that if extra surgery had been necessary, Dr K.K. Madhavan is recognised as the top liver transplant surgeon in the world. My Father had provided the best.

While I was recovering in an 'ordinary' ward, I received a special delivery of some unusual flowers. My friend Warren from London had placed an order to an Edinburgh florist and probably never saw them, which is just as well, because they weren't very pretty. They looked like triffids from John Wyndham's novel. Over the next few days these flowers received more visitors than I did. People would ask me questions about them that I couldn't answer. One night, a ward sister, from another part of the hospital, happened to be passing my ward and she burst into the room with shouts of glee.

'I haven't seen these flowers since I left Africa.' She went on to tell me that they were unique to the Central African Republic (CAR). I burst into tears. Without knowing how ill I was, I had been planning to go to CAR with my World Horizon's friend Rob from the Chateau Blanc in Thumeries, France. Our mission would have coincided with the same date as I was having the liver transplant. It was like God my Father saying, 'You couldn't go there so I sent a little piece of what you missed to you'.

When the transplant team did their ward round later they were all amazed at how well I was doing. All of them recognised God's hand in every detail and in their own words they said, "Your faith has made you well". The transplant took place on April 7th, 2000. My scar looks like I've been sawn in two. Many years have now passed and many subsequent miracles have taken place. I am able to live a very active and healthy life and my regular check-ups at the hospital show that everything is functioning normally. Praise God.

Going back briefly to 'the crows' incident. When we first met Dr K.K. Madhavan he reminded me of a crow, in as much as he had jet-black hair slicked back and an aquiline nose not too unlike a beak. After this, the penny finally dropped and we understood what the Lord was saying to us at that time.

Elijah in the bible (1 Kings 17:6), is instructed to go to the Kerith Ravine where the Lord tells him that ravens (crows) will feed him morning and evening. Ravens (and crows) are carrion birds that eat dead meat and it is forbidden for the Hebrews, according to the Law of Moses, to eat that. In the Bible story, Elijah is being challenged to trust in God and move out of his religious mindset.

God could have supernaturally made food appear, as He did with Manna from heaven with the Israelites in the desert, but he chose not to do that. He provided real meat brought by real birds to keep Elijah alive. God was saying at that time, particularly to Nancy, that He was going to provide an actual liver, from an actual person, and use real people (the Transplant Team) to keep me alive. However, our super-spiritual mindset had to change before we could accept it. Thank God it did!

37

"CLOSE THE BUILDING"

After being discharged from hospital I recovered very well. It is normal procedure for each transplant patient to be intensively followed-up, not just initially but, with less frequency, for the rest of our lives. I am not complaining, I am delighted with the care and attention I receive. In the year 2000, when I received my transplant, liver transplants were still pioneering surgery. At that time only around three people had received a liver transplant.

I was delighted to be back at Kilcreggan House. It had only been six months since the process to purchase the property had started. I had been in hospital for a huge part of that time and Nancy had been with me for most of it. It was a miracle that all the bills were paid. God made some amazing provision at that time.

Just when we needed it, a cheque arrived from my London based photography agency, Rex Features. One of my photographs from years ago had been used as part of a billboard campaign and my commission was £1,500. The Lord used Rex Features frequently to top up our funds when they were depleted. The 'Buy-a-Brick' campaign was still ongoing and the Lord used that to bring us contributions when we most needed them. Of course, at that time there was no conference facilitation for other groups but there were enquiries for bookings and that meant that there was the promise of some money to come in the future.

Most of our trainees were unemployed and many had never worked. In theory we should have been able to claim Housing Benefit for them, but the DHSS (Department of Health and Social Security) system was badly organised, and it usually took months for each claim to be sorted out. Often our trainees would have left before the claim was settled and when they re-registered with the

DHSS in another location, it usually messed-up or stopped the claim for their time with us. Most of the time we gave up just to avoid the hassle, but, occasionally a claim would be settled and that was a great help when it happened.

As the work at Kilcreggan grew and developed so too did the work in Drumchapel. To become a member of the local gang, 'The Peel Glen Boys', or PGB, one of the initiation challenges was for potential members to break into our church building. In the beginning, this would happen at least once every month. We did all we could to stop it; we bricked-up all the ground level windows and put non-drying burglar paint on the edged of our flat roof. It did decrease the number of times when we had to go and clear up the mess, but it didn't stop them trying.

I tried really hard to make our church conform to what the AOG called 'church' but it just wasn't happening. We ran Alpha courses, we had a café on certain days, I started a football team, we had fairly traditional meetings on Sundays but this was not what was needed for the people we worked amongst. In time I became ordained as the Rev. Peter Stanway but the 'church' never was given AOG status. It was becoming clear that our church was more like a 'mission station' than a traditional church.

One night when about seventy of our Children's Church were in the building, rain came in through the damaged flat roof and hit the mains electrical box. There was a flash and all the lights went out, but fortunately, no-one was injured. I set about repairing the damage, replaced the blown fuses and thought to myself, 'that will never happen again'. I was wrong. Exactly the same thing happened the next night and the Lord said to me, 'close the building'.

'Close the building? What would I do if the church closed down?' Yet, I knew God had spoken and that left me no alternative. I had to do what He said, so I closed the building. With a heavy heart, as I pulled down the roller shutter at the front door, God spoke to me again. He said, 'I am giving you a three R's strategy. Not reading, writing and arithmetic like the old school days, these three R's are 'Repair – Rebuild – Renew'.

I took this to be a reference to getting the church building ready to use again; repair – rebuild – renew but, over time, I realised that yes, it was a practical strategy but it also had a deeper spiritual meaning. It refered, initially, to the people, of Drumchapel but later it was to mean all the people that the Lord would send me to all over the world.

We were to 'repair' their broken lives by offering them practical help. We were to 'rebuild' their lack of self-worth by affirming them and giving them hope for the future. We were to 'renew' them by seeing them coming to know Jesus and being born again. However, in the early days, a group of us set about praying for what the Lord was saying about getting the building ready for use.

38

ANOTHER KIND OF POVERTY

During this time, the Lord began to give us favour with the Greggs Bakeries shops. We began to collect unsold food products that they could not keep for re-sale the next day and we distributed these in bags to the people in our area of Drumchapel. At first the people were suspicious, wondering what the 'catch' was, but there was no 'catch'. I had come to know and love these people and the Lord showed me that they were extremely poor. There is a poverty that exists in the Western World that is not created by lack of money but as a result of the misuse of money.

Most of the people we worked amongst were dependent on an unemployment giro-cheque paid to them by the DHSS. Regardless of the amount, more often than not, that giro was spent as soon as it was received. This meant that there was no money left to make ends meet until the next giro came in. Sometimes, in desperation, people would go to a money lender who would charge exorbitant rates of interest on the loan pay back.

When the pressure became too much, those in debt would often turn to alcohol or drugs to alleviate the stress. Of course, this merely compounded the problem often leading to dependency. The pressure from the money lender and pushers (sometimes one and the same person) often led to an 'offer' being made to the debtor. A quantity of drugs would be given to them to sell to settle the outstanding debt that was now, because of super-interest, too high to ever pay back. Due to the debtor's addiction to the drugs that they were supposed to sell they would end up using more than they sold meaning that they were now in even more debt. Now things became really heavy.

Often, in the hope of settling the debt, the debtor was left with no option but to commit a major crime that had been set up by the criminals that they were in debt to; like robbing a bank or post office, settling an old score for them, etc... Other routes would lead to prostitution or trafficking. Therefore, you can see that any help we could give to these desperate people was good.

At that time I enjoyed tremendous favour among the people that I worked with. I had the liberty to open the front door and walk into their homes. They respected me for the work that I was doing and they would often stop what they were doing to talk with me. Many asked me to pray for healing or personal/family problems. Many prayed for salvation. One of the pushers was called Andy and I often visited him at his home. While I was in, there would be a constant knocking on the door. Andy usually sent someone to answer the door and invite the customer to come in. Pretty soon there would be a forlorn looking group of 'rattling' junkies sitting around his living room. They were desperate to score but instead had to endure the conversation I was having with their pusher.

Finally, Andy would suggest, 'Why don't you let the minister pray for you? Peter, why don't you pray for them the way you prayed for me?'
'It's pure dead brilliant' piped-up Sharon, Andy's partner. Before they knew what had hit them, I was praying for each of them and laying hands on them. A tremendous peace came on them and filled the room. They left without their drugs but they did have an encounter with Jesus. I met many of them later on the streets or in other houses and they all remembered the time that we prayed and 'something happened'.

These were not unique occasions. They were part of our every day life and work in Drumchapel. Our children were our ministry team.

Apart from delivering our grocery parcels to the doors up and down the tenement closes they also gathered round to join with me whenever anyone came up to our van for prayer. As the number of bakeries increased we were able to give out enough bags of groceries that would feed up to two hundred families for four or five days each week. We would rotate among families who had the most needs. On the days when we were not distributing groceries we took around cups of soup and bread. Eventually this increased to ten litres of home-made broth, that Nancy made, and many bags of bread each day.

Some families had more than ten children. Many were single-parent families but not all. Most of the people preferred to have a partner, often for security but certainly for companionship. These may have been volatile relationships but they tended to stick together through thick and thin (as was the case with my own parents).

Another factor among the people who made up our congregation was their 'tenement mentality'. Traditionally, Glasgow is a city of red sandstone tenements. On the different landings, or levels, of the three or four floors of the tenements there were three or four apartments. Often all the people who lived in the tenements were related; brothers, sisters, sons, daughters, aunties, uncles, nieces, nephews and cousins, and then there were the half-brothers and half-sisters, etc…

In the 1960's a Government programme was introduced to depopulate the city centre and move the people to a 'green belt' on the city perimeters. At that time Castlemilk, Easterhouse and Drumchapel sprang up. Although there were no tenements, the 'tenement mentality' still prevailed. Now, however, it extended to whole streets. Whenever a house on the street became vacant someone in the family moved quickly to have a family member apply for and usually get the vacant house. This meant that in our catchment area of around two thousand five hundred people there were at most only one hundred families!

This created pros and cons. It was good in the sense that there was no need for fliers to publicise anything. By telling the correct key family members, the word spread like wild fire. On the downside, however, that there were frequent family feuds that led to their own style of 'self policing'. Usually, problems were sorted out within the family but occassionally, this erupted into alcohol and drugs fuelled battles that escalated to all-out war. Machetes and sword-wielding pitched-battles were not uncommon.

After the command to 'close the building', I continued to visit my congregation but I now spent more personal time praying, reading the Bible and listening to God. I was also able to have more quality time with our TFL trainees. Soon, a strategy began to emerge. After specific prayer, I would go to places that had the kind of resources we were looking for; timber, paint, tiles, carpets, fittings, fixtures, etc…. If the person who answered the door to me had the authority to give me what I was looking for then I knew I was in the right place at the right time but, if it was another person, I may have been in the right place but at the wrong time. If that happened, I would politely excuse myself and say I would come back another day.

God blessed us with all kinds of resources. We were able to completely renovate our church building with a new flat roof and a new toilet block with ceiling to floor Italian ceramic tiles and a brand new shower room; a new foyer with pine ceiling and built-in ceiling down-lighters. The main sanctuary was entirely repainted and completely fitted out with brand new carpets throughout the entire building. We decided to give the church a new name, *Drumchapel Community Church*. God was good to us but His provision didn't stop with only what we needed for the church building renovation.

39

"I WILL BLESS YOU"

When Nancy and I first went to minister in Drumchapel, despite the opposition, God gave us a vision for the work. Nancy asked the Lord what 'revival' meant. The Lord showed her a picture of Drumchapel that was in black and white. It showed unkempt gardens with broken toys, dirty windows with curtains askew, impoverished children with raggy clothes but as she watched it was as if someone turned on the colour dial and the gardens looked clean and tidy. The windows had modern blinds and curtains, and the children now dressed in good clothes, looked happy and healthy.

Around the same time the Lord spoke to me about Drumchapel becoming a desirable area with new modern housing and even private housing development where people would buy houses in the area (Isaiah 58:12b.... *you will be called Repairer of Broken Walls, Restorer of Streets with Dwellings.)* While the repair work to our church building was going on it was announced that Drumchapel had been designated as an area of social depravation and as such would become the recipient of multiple millions of pounds of European Social Funding. This money would be used for the building of new homes, schools and recreational facilities. Private developers started to move in and over a five-year period, climaxing in 2005, the transformation of our area made it almost unrecognisable.

During that time, families that were due to move to a brand new home were given a resettlement allowance of around £750. For them, this windfall was like winning the lottery. The money was intended for buying new furniture, carpets and other essential items for their new home. Foolishly, it was given out months before the family were due to move and by the time the move came the money was spent.

While we were renovating the church building it was still closed for public use but our team used it to bag-up the groceries before distribution. As we neared the end of our renovations the resources kept coming in. We realised that these 'extra' resources were to help the families, who had spent their resettlement money, to help them get their new houses equipped for moving in.

God is a God of abundance and using the prayer strategy that the Lord gave us, we found many businesses and businessmen that were very willing to help us. We would always follow-up any help that was given with a 'thank you' letter to the person and place that had helped. We made sure that they knew that we were praying for them to be blessed in accordance with the word of God in Genesis 12:3....... *I will bless those who bless you,...* One such place was a carpet company that provided carpets for large exhibitions at the SECC (Scottish Exhibition and Conference Centre) in Glasgow.

They gave us some 'off-cuts' that were actually enough to carpet our church offices. As was always the case, whatever we were given initially would eventually run out and we would need to go back and ask for more. When I went back to the carpet company, the works manager, Sandie, came up to tell me that the MD, the boss, had received our 'thank you' letter and had instructed him to do anything they could to help us.
'That's nice', I said naively.
'No, you don't understand Peter. I have to do all that I can to help you. Do you know what that means?'
'No,' I said.
'We can give you up to half-a-million-square-meters of carpet every year'....
I tried to imagine what half-a-million-square-meters of carpet would look like. I thought, if half of the population of Glasgow

could gather in one place shoulder to shoulder and chest to back that would be about half-a-million-square-meters. Wow!

From then on we would get a phone call from Sandie saying things like, 'I've got seventeen thousand square meters of carpet from a medical exhibition. They hardly walked on it, do you want it?' The trouble was that all the carpet had to be collected almost immediately and it had to be stored by us. I hired a twelve-by-twenty feet steel shipping container and had it positioned on the edge of our church car park. When a collection was due I called on everyone I could to help and we ferried the carpets from Finnieston to Drumchapel sometimes in a hired van but more often in our little white mini-bus.

Word quickly spread and we ended up helping Social Work clients all over Glasgow as well as giving carpets to churches and community projects all over Scotland. In Drumchapel we completely carpeted more than six hundred and fifty homes for free.

After a year of going in and out to B&Q, (the DIY hardware store), they designated a corner of their yard for us. I would drive in once every week and collect whatever was there. They gave us pallets of paint, ceramic tiles, bathroom suites and much more. More and more Drumchapel Community Church was looking less and less like a traditional church.

I became the chaplain of the largest primary school in Drumchapel, Pinewood Primary School. I was invited every week to take the assembly. I had a great relationship with Moira the Headmistress. We both loved the children and we had an insight into their needs and backgrounds. I was invited to the teacher's 'In Service' days whenever there was any special training being done so that we all moved forward together with the same children. Unfortunately, after a year or so, Moira had an accident that kept her off school for three months. In her absence the Deputy Head made changes that affected my situation there and when Moira returned it was evident that she was being forced to stop working with our church.

40

TOUGH

Declan was about five years old when I met first met him. He was a hyper active, cheeky child whose parents had been drug addicts for around seventeen years at that time. Declan's dad was in jail for a crime he didn't commit (armed robbery of the ice cream van) but didn't mind because it made up for the times that he had not been jailed for the crimes he did commit.

Declan stole some money out of his mum's purse and bicycled to McDonald's in Clydebank (a distance of about three miles each way in busy traffic). He wanted to buy himself a Happy Meal. Who can blame him? I was able to visit Andy (that's right, Andy the pusher from a few pages back) in jail almost every month and we did bible studies together. He was drug free and fit. When he came out of jail after nearly four years it only took about three days before he went straight back to his old way of life.

He managed to get a job as a watchman with the security firm who had been given the responsibility to look after the sites where the new building work was going on. One night, to shelter from the cold, he climbed the few steps ascending into the watchman's hut. He had been silently followed, was pushed in and stabbed with a sword that went in through his side and out of his arm pit. He died twice due to loss of blood on the way to the hospital. When Nancy and I went up to see him in hospital the next day he was standing outside in the freezing cold wearing a hospital gown and foam slippers smoking a roll-up (a make-your-own cigarette). Drumchapel folk are tough. They are a different breed.

Similarly, the children could be found out playing in all weathers the boys wearing only a t-shirt and jeans and the girls wore little skimpy dresses. They didn't ever seem to feel or catch the cold.

There were two shifts in Drumchapel; the late shift and the night shift. The late shift were the children who go out to play when they come home from school. There would be children and youth hanging around the streets, younger boys playing football or girls with their dolls and prams. Around midnight, the late shift disappeared making way for the night shift who come out to play. Children and youth loitered around the streets, younger boys playing football or girls with their dolls and prams. The ice cream van went around the scheme (the housing estate) all night. There was no early shift.

Johnny was first brought to the church by the police. They had found him on the streets playing truant from school. At the age of eleven, Johnny had only been to school for a total of seven months. We started to teach Johnny from the ACE curriculum that we used with Israel, but he couldn't settle. One night, when we were just about to go home, Johnny ran up to the church in a panic. He told us that we needed to come to his house right away.

Linzi, Johnny's mum, along with Johnny's older brother and sister were living in a derelict building and were the only occupants in the close. The original occupants had been 'decanted' in preparation to be moved into a new house. She was there in protest because she was unhappy with the house that the council had offered her. It wasn't a new house but her old house that had been redecorated after a fire. There was no electricity in the close so the power for her electric fire, cooker and lighting came from a cable rigged-up to the street light outside.

Her door had been kicked-in so frequently that there was no point in fitting a lock any more. That night she had been visited by a freaky heavy guy who demanded to know where her ex-boyfriend was. Linzi said she didn't know and this heavy started to slap her face and threatened her saying that she had half-an-hour to remember and then he would be back. She could hear him going down the stairs laughing with his friends in the darkness. She thought to herself, going back into the light, I must have been really nervous, I'm sweating. As she wiped her face her hands were covered in blood. As he slapped her, this beast had been slashing her with a blade. She washed herself down. At this point Johnny came home.

Before she had time to pull herself together, she heard shuffling and sardonic laughter on the landing in the close. She ran to the kitchen and picked up the deep fat fryer that had been switched on the whole time heating the oil for chips It was now boiling and she ran to the door just as her unwelcome visitor pushed it open. She threw the oil full force all over him. He took off racing down the stairs, this time not laughing but screaming.

Johnny was sent to get me. Nancy and I rushed to see Linzi. We did our best to comfort her and we prayed for her. She accepted Jesus that night. Within a week or so, Linzi and the whole family were re-housed in another part of Drumchapel.

41

PEOPLE AND PLACES

Drumchapel was in a state of constant flux, people were always coming and going at a tremendous rate. Sadly, people died far too often, sometimes through an accidental overdose, murder or suicide. Jim and Robert were brothers aged eleven and nine respectively. They were great helpers with the grocery work, always among the first at the door waiting to unload the bakery trays. They were fast with the bagging up and the deliveries. They were lovely boys with a good attitude. Over a period of about two months we saw them every day that we were in Drumchapel, then they disappeared. I made enquiries and discovered that they were staying with their auntie in England. One night they had gone home after church and found their dad hanging dead, with a rope around his neck, in the kitchen. Sad, very sad.

On another day, when I was leaving the school after an assembly, I noticed a policeman and a policewoman, in the middle of a patch of grass, with some blue and white police tape blowing in the wind. On further inspection, I noticed that there was a semi-naked male body lying dead at their feet on the ground. I phoned the school and told them to keep the children back until the body had been removed. There was no discreet white tent here, the body was clear for all to see. These events were all too common, so much so that what used to be front page news in the national press, didn't even reach the local newspaper.

Sometimes, I went to visit old Matt, I would find, among the people who gathered in his 'drinking den', Donna and her two beautiful young daughters, one aged two and the other still in a pram. Donna was an alcoholic and she loved her children, but the demon of alcohol had its claws deep into her. The Social Work Department eventually took her children into care. Donna was distraught and hated the Social Workers, whom she blamed, as did most of the people in Drumchapel. They almost all lived in constant fear that their children would be taken into care.

Natalie became pregnant to a boyfriend who didn't want to know. She seriously considered having an abortion and made plans to do so. On the night before the termination, Natalie had a dream in which I told her not to have the abortion. I heard this story for the first time as I bounced healthy little Emma in her bouncy baby chair. I burst into tears at the thought that she could have been another victim of needless death in Drumchapel.

William and his brother murdered a boy in broad daylight. They beat him to death with a baseball bat. It was witnessed by many people. They were guilty. They were released from custody on bail. Whilst awaiting trial, William lost the plot. He spent most of his time out of his mind with drugs and alcohol. Often, when he was wrecked, he would walk into people's houses, unplug their TV and/or video, (sometimes while they were watching it) and walk back out with it under his arm to sell for more drugs and alcohol. He was hated by the community and he was hated by the police but William couldn't care less.

When he was too stoned to stand, people would take their opportunity to give vent to their hatred. William's face and body was full of stab wounds and slashes. I often saw him wandering the streets of Drumchapel. One day while I was out delivering groceries, he came up to our mini-bus and asked for prayer. We all gathered around him and prayed. He started to cry and fell down under the power of the Holy Spirit. The time came for the trial at which William and his brother were found not-guilty. No-one, including William, could believe it.

For those boys who wanted help, but were still active addicts, we worked closely with a rehab centre that was part of Teen Challenge

(TC); The Haven, Kilmacolm in the hills behind Greenock. Early one morning, I was picking up Nathan to take him there when William showed up and asked if he could go too. I took both of them with me so that they could be assessed at the same time, but I knew that they would not taken-in together. This was because they were two people from the same area who knew each other. Both were assessed and Nathan was offered a place in the Haven immediately and William was offered a place in Teen Challenge, London.

We booked a ticket and arranged for him to be collected at the other end and much to everyone's surprise he turned up and started the programme. He lasted for over 18 months during which time he was transferred to the Teen Challenge main base in Wales. He came back to Scotland for court appearances, for misdemeanours from the past, and when he did, he stayed with us at Kilcreggan House. He was getting his life into order until he met a girl at TC Wales and ran away with her. He eventually split with her and ended-up back in Drumchapel.

Nathan didn't last at The Haven. He left after a few days and came back to Drumchapel where he stayed with his mum Leah. Nancy and I visited Leah regularly. She first came to the church for Nathan's baptism and we maintained contact. She was dependent on prescribed drugs. For one brief spell she had a boyfriend and ended up pregnant. When her daughter Lily was born she was blind and was immediately taken into care. Leah had two other young children, Justin, about twelve years old and Kayla, ten. They were both already in care. Nathan was the youngest of three grown-up brothers. Nathan was the one that the police arrested whenever they weren't sure who was guilty of a crime in the area. The chances were that he was involved in some way. This meant that he spent a considerable time in prison yet, at heart, Nathan was a good boy. Imagine my surprise when years later Nathan phoned me up to tell me that he was now drug free. He wanted to get married and asked if I 'would I do the honours'. What a privilege, I said, 'definitely, yes!' He is now happily married.

Ella and Jack were the only couple ever to be married by me in the church building in Drumchapel. They were a great couple who had a young, hyper active toddler, also called Jack. Ella would bring wee Jack to the church every Sunday and she was a great helper with the grocery distribution. Her husband Jack was a drug addict who was on a methadone programme. Ella was not a drug addict but she pretended to be in order for her to go onto a methadone programme too to boost what Jack was receiving. Over a period of years Ella did become a drug addict and it led to her and Jack splitting up. Just days before she was due to go to a rehab centre in England she killed herself by jumping from the window of the high flats, where she was living. It was very tragic and the funeral was traumatic.

42

BACKSLIDING COULD COST YOU YOUR EARS

Ethan turned up out of the blue. He was a Drumchapel boy who was saved as a youth in the local Church of Scotland in Drumchapel. He met an American girl, Angela, who was part of a mission from the USA to that church. They fell in love and later Ethan went to the States and they were married. Shortly after the birth of their third child, Angela died and Ethan came back to Scotland with his three children.

Ethan and the children moved in with his friend, Jacob, who lived in our part of Drumchapel and all of them started to attend Drumchapel Community Church. Ethan was becoming increasingly more involved with the work at the church and was leaving the children in the care of Jacob more often. This was putting a lot of pressure on Jacob who had no previous experience with children. Sadly, it wasn't too long before Jacob, followed by Nathan, backslid into their old way of life. One night Ethan and Jacob went on a bender and ended-up in a drugs and alcohol induced stupor. They argued and fell out. Jacob went home first and when Ethan tried to get in later, Jacob attacked him and bit-off both his ears. Jacob ended up in a locked psychiatric ward and Ethan went through many months of trauma counselling. Ethan came to Kilcreggan for a period of time, something that his parents gladly encouraged and they looked after his children to allow him the freedom to do so. He went through the TFL course.

Eventually, Ethan became a graduate of Andrew Womack's Bible College in England. While he was there he met another student, Sophia, from Hungary and they were married. They now minister together for the glory of God. However, it is worth remembering that backsliding can cost you your ears....

Richard was my constant companion during all the outreach in Drumchapel. He started working with me when he was twelve years old and stayed with me all the way through. He had all the makings of becoming a Pastor. He was a lovely boy, level headed and hard working. He loved helping me and he was developing a great relationship with Jesus. He wanted to be a policeman when he left school but failed the entrance exam, so he started working in Farmfoods and became the manager of the Drumchapel store. He settled down with a nice girl and shares a flat with his sister and her child. I am sure God will use Richard for His glory. I try to stay in touch with him and his mother.

Gertie loved me. She first came to our church, via the Salvation Army, with her friend Mary. Mary played the piano and Gertie sang. They were great friends. Not long after I baptised them, Mary missed a few events at our church and Gertie became concerned. There was no answer at the door of her house and the police were alerted. Sadly, we found Mary dead in her chair.

Even as the police were taking statements, Gertie was careful to avoid giving her age. She was very theatrical, flamboyant and somewhat eccentric. When it came to the time for her to be re-housed, she reluctantly agreed to allow me to help move her belongings. She had warned me about her doll collection.
'It can't be that bad', I said. 'Where are they?'
Just down the hall, the last room on the right.' Nothing could have prepared me for what I was about to see. I opened the door and stepped in. I felt like an intruder barging unannounced into their private world. Over three hundred pairs of eyes trans-fixed with their gaze. All of them put on a brave smile. I felt like apologising. Some where standing, some sitting; one played the piano, another was dressed as a bride.

When Gertie died, I had the honour of conducting her funeral. As the pall-bearers carried in her coffin, I almost expected to see a trail of sequins flow behind them! We were all shocked to discover her true age, more than twenty years older than she told us. However, I can't tell you what age she was, that's her secret.

From time to time, people would tell me that I was wasting my time, working with all those 'wasters' in Drumchapel, but I knew that God had placed me there. I recognised that those who became Christians did not always conform to the popular image of what Christians should be like. Sometimes, their lifestyle did dot change all that noticeably, but I knew that they had experienced a genuine encounter with God and that the process of sanctification had started. I am convinced that I will meet many of my Drumchapel congregation in heaven.

We had many water baptisms in our baptismal tank in Drumchapel. We made each one into a special event and invited all the friends and family of every candidate to come along. We would baptise, on average, six Christian believers every two weeks, many of whom were school children. The requirement for baptism was that the person was born again and fully understood what they were doing.

Once, a boy aged around eight or nine years old, whom I had never seen before, came along to one of our baptism events with a towel under his arm.
'Hi, what's your name?' I asked him.
'Lucas' he replied.
'What brings you here tonight Lucas?'
'I'm going to be baptised', he said proudly.
'Do you know anyone here?' I enquired
'My cousin, Sandra. She was baptised last time and told me all about it.'
I found Sandra, a charming girl about eleven years old, and asked her to tell her cousin Lucas all about Jesus. About ten minutes later, Sandra brought Lucas up to me and said, 'He wants to get

saved.' I led Lucas to the Lord there and then and he was baptised with the others that night.

Tommy Thomson first came to join us at the Bible College in Drumchapel in 1997. He went on to become a TFL trainee at Kilcreggan House and then he was my Children's Director for the Children's Church in Drumchapel. Tommy was a professional Christian clown known as *Clownbo*. He regularly helped with the food distribution. Tommy was generosity personified and between us we came up with some ground-breaking and innovative ways of reaching the children with the gospel and the love of Jesus Christ.

Children's Church was our work-out time and we would run around crazy with them for two hours. During that time we would also have 'quiet times' when the children, sometimes up to seventy of them in one session, would lie on their backs, catch their breath and listen to God speak to them. I would ask them what He said. Some of the responses would come back,
'I love you.'
'You are special.'

Most of our children came from difficult family backgrounds and grew up in homes where there was little or no order or discipline. Sometimes, when they were very badly behaved and disruptive at church we had to resist the temptation to send them home. That would not have been a satisfactory solution. It would have been yet another rejection in their chaotic young lives.

We came up with a better solution. Like football, they were given a yellow card that meant sitting-out of the game they were playing. A second yellow card meant sitting-out for the rest of the evening's activities. A red card meant missing the following week at the Children's Church. This system was seen by all to be fair and it worked well.

When the children did well they were rewarded with 'Jesus money', which was mock money made to look like a dollar bill with the face of Jesus on it. They were given these for good behaviour, good attendance, good team work, etc… and once a month they could spend their Jesus money in 'The Children's Church Shop'. Tommy bought a selection of good items during the run up to each month's shop and the children could 'buy' CD players, the latest music CDs, quality games, sweets and toys.

Another of my committed helpers was Isabel. She was a middle-aged woman who first came to the church to ask us to pray for her son, Joe, who was in prison for serious assault. He was a drug addict. Isabel continued to come to church and began to help me with the groceries, the soup round and in any way she could…

When Joe came out of prison he attended our church in Drumchapel, where he gave his life to Jesus, and later joined us at Kilcreggan House as a TFL trainee. He stayed with us for two years and did very well. The people who knew him from Drumchapel were amazed at the change. As the time approached for us to prepare Joe for going back into the 'jungle', he began to get itchy feet and wanted to leave before he was ready. One morning after an argument, he left taking two other boys with him. After two weeks back in Drumchapel he was dabbling with drugs again and before long he had a full-on drug habit.

How can this happen? Well, the devil obviously hated Joe and his powerful Christian testimony. The devil's mission is to *'steal and kill and destroy'* the life of every believer (John 10:10). A tactic that he uses to do this is to hold us back from God's perfect timing by tempting Christians to procrastinate or, alternatively, to push us forward too fast until we get ahead of God's plan. In both scenarios we miss the mark and we miss God's best for us. God wants to work all things together for our good so that, at the optimum time, we will have the maximum blessing. The devil, who works through our mind, will and emotions, will do all he can to prevent us from entering into God's best.

Whenever trainees left the church or Kilcreggan House for the wrong reasons we would normally take them back if they asked. Sadly, no-one ever really made a go of it the second time and some would even try a third time. Many who never made it ended up dead or in prison. I am often asked, 'How come you made it?' and all I can answer is, 'There, but for the grace of God, go I.'

43

"LET HIM GO"

While I was in hospital for my first liver biopsy and check-up in April 2001, Jim Baxter the famous Glasgow Rangers and Scotland football player was admitted to the bed next to mine. He had been diagnosed with liver cancer and this had also affected his pancreas making him diabetic. He was struggling with how to give himself injections so, I asked him if he wanted help. This got us talking to each other and we chatted for a little while until I had to go for a shower.

While I was in the shower I prayed and asked the Lord how I might witness to Jim and I believe that the Lord put on my heart to tell him about the thief on the cross. It was coming up to Easter and the time when even non-Christians become conscious that Easter was the time of the crucifixion of Jesus. I came out of the shower and sat on the edge of my bed facing Jim. He already knew I was a minister.

'Have you ever read the bible, Jim?' I asked him.
'No, I can't understand it with all that old-fashioned language like 'thee' and 'thou''I explained to him, 'Nowadays there are modern translations that use the kind of English that we're speaking right now. Do you want to see?' I passed him my NIV (New International Version) copy of the Bible. I had already found the passage I wanted and said, 'There you go Jim, read that to me'.
Jim began to read, 'One of the criminals who hung there hurled insults at him: "Aren't you the Christ? Save yourself and us!"
But the other criminal rebuked him. "Don't you fear God," he said, "since you are under the same sentence? We are punished justly, for we are getting what our deeds deserve. But this man has done nothing wrong."

Then he said, "Jesus, remember me when you come into your kingdom." Jesus answered him, "I tell you the truth, today you will be with me in paradise."'

Jim slammed the Bible shut, thrust it back into my hands, and rushed away to the toilet. I prayed that Jim would understand that, despite this hedonistic lifestyle that he bragged about, it was never too late to ask for forgiveness and receive Jesus into his heart. A few short days after this Jim Baxter died.

After my second annual liver biopsy, it was discovered that my new liver was becoming infected by the Hepatitis virus. I was offered a course of Interferon/Ribavirin treatment and the doctors explained, in detail, all the negative side-effects to expect if I accepted the offer. There was no way that I wanted to go through this treatment. I prayed and wrestled with it until, finally, in January 2003 I decided to give it a go.

On the morning that I was scheduled to receive my first injection, the Lord spoke to me though John 11:44 .... *The dead man came out, his hands and feet wrapped with strips of linen, and a cloth around his face. Jesus said to them, "Take off the grave clothes and let him go."*

The dead man came out, his hands and feet wrapped with strips of linen, and a cloth around his face. Without miraculous intervention, I was a 'dead man'. The shroud of death; the 'strips of linen' and the 'cloth' that bound me represented Hepatitis C. Jesus commanded that these 'grave clothes' be removed, taken off, and that I was to be 'let go'.

Immediately, I knew deep in my spirit, that God had intervened and that Jesus had commanded my healing. I, therefore, went to that first hospital appointment with a spring in my step and told the

Hep. C team that, although I was going to go through the treatment, I fully believed that I was already healed.

Three months into the treatment the 'viral load test' result stated, 'no virus found'. However, the doctors insisted that I complete the twelve months course. During that time none of the major side-effects (hair loss, anxiety, psychosis, depression, etc) affected me. Towards the end I did become quite tired, worn-out and emotional but not to the extent that I was told to expect. I finished the treatment at the end of January 2004 but had to wait another six months for the final tests to be completed.

In July 2004 I was told that the Hepatitis C was gone.
I said, 'Can it come back?'
'No', they said, 'go and have a long, healthy and happy life.'
'Praise God! You must be delighted to give people this fantastic news', I exclaimed.
'Well…actually, you are the first patient ever, post transplant, to be completely healed.'
'This is a miracle, praise God!' I shouted
'Yes, this is wonderful' exclaimed the nurse. 'Your faith has made the difference.'

Romans 10:17 (KJV) says ...... *So then faith cometh by hearing, and hearing by the word of God.*

It was around this time that the Lord began to speak to me about releasing the work in Drumchapel. At first I didn't believe it was God that I was hearing, I thought that it was the devil trying to steal the work. I began to rebuke God thinking He was the devil. How could it be God? This was one of our most fruitful periods out of all our time in Drumchapel. The Lord said, 'Take this model out into the world.' Finally, after a few months, I began to realise that it was indeed God who was speaking and, in obedience, I began to let go of the work.

Over the next year I looked for people who could continue with the work. Isabel and Richard knew the ropes thoroughly. Archie could drive and the volunteers would be happy to help. Unfortunately however, with Drumchapel being as unstable as it is and drama being a constant factor, what I left behind was to fizzle-out as a physical entity and our Drumchapel Community Church building eventually became a funeral parlour - sadly, a business in great demand. The year was 2005.

Something powerful happened to me two weeks after I stopped my work in Drumchapel. It confirmed to me that I had heard correctly from God. I decided to go back just to see what was going on. I parked my familiar white minibus outside of Richard's house and almost immediately children came running from all directions to see me. 'Any cakes Peter?' they asked. They were in the front of the van, the back of the van all over the place and for the first time ever, I panicked. Already there were new faces, unfamiliar to me, looking out at me from the houses. If I didn't know them then they didn't know me. What would they be thinking? Who is this guy in the van with children all around him?

I quickly emptied the van of all the children, locked the doors and drove away. 'What happened there, Lord?' I enquired.
'You had no anointing. You no longer need the anointing you once had because you are no longer called to work here.' He answered.
Then I realised that for the eight years I had been working in Drumchapel with the 'undesirables' of Glasgow, I had never once felt fear. The tremendous favour that I had in their home and on the streets was because of God's anointing upon me for the job he had given me to do. In a paradoxical way, now that the anointing was gone, I knew that I was no longer meant to be there.

Although the physical work disappeared, I am convinced that the work that was done for the kingdom of God has eternal value. We did impact many people's lives and Jesus was invited into many hearts. We still hear, on the jungle telegraph, news of what is happening in Drumchapel and I, occasionally, meet some of my former congregation. Like I said before, I am expecting to meet quite a number of people from Drumchapel when we all get to heaven.

44

BACK AT KILCREGGAN HOUSE

As I said before, we often had had special Teaching Seminars for our TFL trainees and among the invited teachers were Judith Butler and Rauna May. At that time Rauna was Hector Gimenez's Translator and International Director but she later went to join Wayne Cordeiro at New Hope Hawaii as one of their Pastors. Out of the blue in 2002 Rauna announced that she thought it would be good for me to go to the Leaders Practicum in Hawaii and she would pay for all the expenses!

Going to Hawaii was an awesome experience, not so much because of its outstanding beauty, but more for the people I met and the Practicum itself. The Practicum was a look-over-the-shoulder of the leaders at New Hope Hawaii and an insight into how they all worked together to make it a huge success. In fact, the Pastor, Wayne Cordeiro, has written a book called, 'Doing Church as a Team'. Above all, the concept of 'journaling', that I learned during this time eventually morphed into my weekly worldwide teaching called the 'Gist'.

By now, the primary focus for the work at Kilcreggan House was running it as a Conference Centre. We still had trainees and volunteers but the main emphasis was to facilitate conferences for other church organisations and groups. The Church on the Rock that met at Kilcreggan House continued to do so but it was becoming increasingly more difficult for us to meet. Incidentally, in old Scots language, 'Kilcreggan' means 'church on the rock'. At our peak we would have a conference every weekend. Sometimes more than one group held a conference at the same time. It was very hard work! Nancy was the General Manager and also the 'chief cook and bottle washer'.

With her gift of hospitality and her eye for detail, Nancy re-styled the house. She, sometimes assisted by Anna and Linsey, two of our trainee volunteers, made all the curtains and the bed-spreads. Her menus and presentation were first class and she quickly gained a reputation that brought our guests back again and again. Kilcreggan House became known as a Centre of Excellence. We adopted a 'guest of honour' principle and served every guest as though they were Jesus Himself. Thanks to these elements and the Lord's tremendous favour, Kilcreggan House became the most popular Conference Centre in Scotland at that time.

Towards the end of 2003, Revelation TV, a Christian satellite TV station invited me to be interviewed by their founder Howard Conder. It was an hour long programme and a great experience.

Around this time an amazing thing happened to us. We had been to my sister's house in Carmunnock for a family meal on the lead-up to Christmas. It was quite late in the evening when we left to drive the ninety minutes journey back to Kilcreggan. On the way home it began to snow and, the further away we travelled away from the city, the snow became heavier and lay deeper on the ground. By the time we reached the steep incline from Rosneath up to Kilcreggan the snow was more than six inches deep.

Due to the lateness of the hour and the adverse weather conditions there were no other cars on the road, no tyre tracks to follow up the steep hill. Half way up our car wheels started to skid and we had to stop. What were we to do? Both of us were dressed for a night out and not equipped to walk over the hills in deep snow.

Suddenly, there was a knock on Nancy's window, she lowered it and a friendly voice took us aback. He said, 'Put the car into first gear and gently move forward.' Our rescuer went to the back of the car and started to push. Slowly, we inched our way up the hill until we reached the crest. When we were safe and on the downward slope we looked back to see our helper, but he was gone. We didn't search for him. It was late so, praising God, we made our way home.

However, when we thought about this incident, there was no way that any person could have pushed a car with three passengers up a steep hill in six inches of snow. We are convinced that God sent an angel to rescue us.

In autumn 2004, Nancy and I were invited to attend the first Master's Commission International Network Conference in Copenhagen. We had already hosted Master's Commission groups at Kilcreggan House and we believed that they were an excellent organisation. The very first Master's Commission began in 1985 in Phoenix, Arizona USA. It emerged as a distinct youth work with its own identity from Phoenix First Assembly (AOG) where Tommy Barnett was the Senior Pastor. Students dedicated one year of their life to scripture memory, study of the word, and ministry.

Nancy and I had previously visited the first Dream Centre in Los Angeles, California in spring 2004. It is a fantastic place that offers multi-faceted Christian discipleship. The vision was given to Tommy Barnett and his son Matthew, who is the current Director. We were excited about the prospect of working closely with Master's Commission and we were prepared to host the first Scottish Master's Commission in Kilcreggan House, 'MC Scotland'.

While we were in Copenhagen, the Coordinator for Assemblies of God Church Planting in Europe and CEO of Master's Commission Europe had arranged a meeting of the newly formed group of Trustees for MC Scotland. Invited to that meeting were the Superintendent of the AOG in Scotland and members of the Scottish Regional Executive Council (REC), myself and Nancy.

Disappointingly, the meeting went badly and, deep in my heart, I knew that I would have no more involvement with the MC Scotland Board. A few weeks after returning to Scotland, I submitted my carefully worded letter of resignation to the MC Scotland Trustees which they accepted.

45

THE HOLY LAND

May 2004 was Nancy's fiftieth birthday and I wanted to do something special for her. Revelation TV had put together a five day tour of the Holy Land to coincide with the Feast of Pentecost. We went and were rewarded with some unforgettable experiences. It changed our lives and put within us a deep love for Israel. We went as part of the first ever group arranged through Revelation TV and it turned out to be the largest ever tour group from the UK. There were three aeroplanes and thirteen coaches involved. It was only for five days but we probably squeezed ten days worth of sight-seeing into those five days! It was exhausting but our adrenalin sustained us.

On the night before we were due to start our journey, Tim Vince, the tour operator, phoned and asked me if I would consider being a bus Pastor. After consulting with Nancy, I agreed. My duties included; starting each day with prayer, keeping the passengers on my bus up-to-date on any new or change of plans and keeping them together at the different sites we visited. I encouraged people to share testimonies on the bus each day. I also arranged for baptisms and rededications that would take place on the day that we visited Yardenit, the baptismal site on the River Jordan. I had the honour of doing the baptisms.

We covered the length and breadth of the country of Israel and it was amazing. As we were there at the time of the Feast of Pentecost, some of the people on my bus had asked me to pray for them to be baptised in the Holy Spirit in the Upper Room in Jerusalem. This was the place where a public baptism in the Holy Spirit had first begun with the original disciples of Jesus and their families - all one hundred and twenty people who were gathered there. It was the fulfilment of a prophecy by Joel in the Bible:

Joel 2:28-29….. I will pour out my Spirit on all people. Your sons and daughters will prophesy, your old men will dream dreams, your young men will see visions. Even on my servants, both men and women, I will pour out my Spirit in those days.

I was completely unprepared for what was going to happen. A small group of us gathered in the Upper Room and I began to anoint them with oil and pray (quite quietly) for them to be filled with the Holy Spirit. Some of them began to fall down onto the floor and rest in the Spirit whilst others began to speak in tongues. The next thing we knew was the sound of 'Thud! Thud! Thud!' We turned, and saw that the sounds were coming from an approaching Greek Orthodox group all with long grey beards and dressed head to foot in black flowing robes. They were thumping their ornate sticks on the floor.

'Get out of here!' their leader said with his eyes popping and veins bulging.

'No', I calmly replied. 'We have as much right to be here as you'.

He pushed his face right into mine, 'What is your name?' he asked, spitting venomously. I told him and he ordered one of his group to video me 'for evidence'. Evidence of what I have no idea but, for one fleeting moment, I had a glimpse of what it may have been like for Jesus when he was confronted by the Pharisees.

The following year, in June 2005, Nancy, our son Israel and I returned to the Holy land and this time we also took Samuel. Israel and Samuel both paid their own way through sponsorship that they managed to raise.

Samuel was a young man who had faithfully worked with me in Drumchapel. He lived on his own and was going through a divorce from his first wife who was a prostitute. They had two children who had been taken into care. Samuel's house was in one of the worst parts of 'the Glen' (Drumchapel) and a gang of troublesome youths would often terrorise him. They would frequently kick-in his door to the point where there were no longer any locks on it. The PGB (Peel Glen Boys) would use his house as a drinking den or shooting gallery and Samuel had no authority over them.

It all came to a head when, whilst working on one of the security sites, Samuel caught some of the youths stealing. They threatened to kill him, so for his protection he came to live at Kilcreggan House and became a TFL trainee. During the two years Samuel was with us he was dramatically transformed in every way; physically, physiologically and spiritually. One of his highlights was coming with us to the Holy Land. I had the privilege of baptising Samuel in the River Jordan.

46

NEPAL

In October 2005 I set off on my first mission to Nepal. I met Pastor Krishna at Kingdom Faith Roffey in 1995 when he came to be a student there. We had kept in touch since that time. In fact Pastor Krishna took our model for WOTS in Scotland and called it WOTS in Nepal. Over the years Pastor Krishna (whom I called 'Kris') was to become our friend and he visited us in Scotland and in Drumchapel several times. He came to regard me as a 'father-figure'. I asked my friend, Pastor Donnie if he wanted to accompany me to Nepal and he readily agreed.

Kris had, by this time, established an orphanage and a church in the capital city, Kathmandu. Pastor Donnie and I lived in a small room in the orphanage. We shared the building with around twenty orphaned children as well as Kris, his wife Pabitra and their two sons. We couldn't travel far from Kathmandu because, at that time, there was political trouble with Maoist Communist insurgents and the Nepalese Army had placed checkpoints and blockades all around the city.

One day we did manage to go a little way up into the mountains where, in an ice cold crystal clear river, we secretly baptised some recent converts from Pastor Krishna's New Life Church. Most of our ministry took place in that church. However, on another day, while it was still dark, we climbed up into another part of the mountains where we watched the sunrise come up behind the Himalayas. It was spectacular.

Nepal is a fascinating place but the politics over the past few years have sent it spiralling backwards into the dark ages. I believe that it all started when almost all of the members of the royal family were massacred at the hands of Crown Prince Dipendra in, June 2001.

What I have just said is controversial and still unproven although, it is widely regarded as the truth. This made a way for Gyanendra to become king. Numerous theories suggest that masked men dressed up as the Crown Prince committed the murders, and it is widely believed that Prince Gyanendra was responsible; suspected but never proven.

In 2008, King Gyanendra was forced to stand down under pressure from a multi-party coalition government that was 'controlled' by the Maoist Communists. Since then the social, political and economic state of the country has worsened. With embargos on the Nepalese borders, food is scarce. The rolling blackouts, also referred to as load shedding, result in frequent intentionally-engineered power cuts.

The Nepalese people are resourceful and are not easily stopped. Although there are strongly enforced curfews in the evenings, Christians continue to meet for fellowship whenever they can. Fuel for vehicles, cooking and heating is scarce and the petrol is rationed to one litre per vehicle at a time. This results in constant queues at armed petrol stations. These queues can be up to one mile long. To get round this people often burn low grade fuel in their vehicles. This makes Kathmandu, even at four thousand three hundred and forty-four feet above sea level, one of the most polluted cities in the world.

Before returning to Scotland, I wanted to purchase some goods that I could sell to raise funds for the work in Nepal. Kris took us to his jeweller friend where he had lodged when he first came to Kathmandu as a student. I asked him if he could make us fifty simple silver crosses. I drew the design and he told us to come back the next day. When we returned we were ushered upstairs to the family's cramped living quarters to see and pay for our order. Suddenly my mind flashed to a scene from the movie 'Midnight Express' as the low sunlight slanted through the dusty dark room suspending time for a transitory moment. I smiled silently myself as we inspected the little plastic bags that contained crosses of pure silver thinking how, in another life, this could have been the setting for an illegal drugs deal if I had never met Jesus Christ at Calvary's Cross.

We had an awesome time in Nepal and I began to see how the Lord might use our Christian Discipleship resources there and in other countries. Our 'Foundations' course would be a great introduction into TFL (Training for Life) but, I realised, it would need to be translated. Therefore, soon after returning to Scotland I began to prepare the Training for Life course for an international audience.

Kris followed-up our mission with a request for us to take his brother Silas as a TFL trainee at Kilcreggan House. We agreed but, after only a couple of weeks, Silas absconded and ended up in Sweden where he currently lives. He used us to get himself out of Nepal. Who can blame him knowing what life is like there? Kris and all his family were horrified at what Silas had done but it didn't stop him asking me if I could take another brother, Bishwa, in his place. We agreed and Bishwa came to stay and train with us for six months.

While he was with us, as well as completing the TFL course, Bishwa also translated our Foundations course into Nepali. He returned to Nepal in the springtime of 2007 and a month or so later I followed this up with our second mission to Nepal.

During all this time the work was developing and growing at Kilcreggan House and so too was our new, expanding, international ministry. I began to look for translators for our weekly teaching, the Gist, and one by one I found them. I started work on a website that would offer our free Christian Discipleship resources; www.thewaycm.com was soon receiving more than one million visits annually. Through our website, invitations to visit and to minister began to come in from all over the world. I needed to quickly learn which of them were genuine.

In sharp contrast to my missions to Third World countries, in 2005 I was invited to speak at a Christian Discipleship School near Cannes in the South of France. This was to become an annual event. Nancy and I (and Israel on occasion) stayed with Vladimir at his beautiful work-in-progress house in Vallauris. He was to become my good friend.

47

KENYA

I began to plan the next mission, this time to Africa; more specifically to Kenya and Rwanda. I planned it for June 2006 one year after I began communicating, via the Internet, with pastors in those countries. This time I was going on my own. I was moving into uncharted waters and I thought it best if I blaze the trail first, and for the next trip I would take others with me. What an eventful mission it turned out to be!

I landed at Jomo Kenyatta International Airport in Nairobi, Kenya. There I was met by my contact Festus and his friend Pastor Chuma. I was taken to Pastor Chuma's house near the airport. After visiting the church and ministering there we went back to the house and slept. The next day I caught a flight from Nairobi to Kisumu. Pastor Chuma and Festus drove to Kisumu in Pastor Chuma's car. We were going to meet at the airport and from there I was to be driven to our Evangelistic Outreach Event at Omoringamu near Ogembo in Kisii Lands.

Unknown to me, some of the leaders from Ogembo were also driving in a 'matatu' (a taxi minibus) to meet me at Kisumu Airport. The race was on between the two vehicles to see who would reach me first. They both reached me almost at the same time and there was a heated argument about who would take me to Omoringamu. I went with the matatu but almost immediately it had a blow out resulting in a flat tyre. I transferred to Pastor Chuma's car. After a treacherous drive despite Pastor Chuma's great driving skills, we all arrived in Ogembo at the same time. Pastor Chuma, Festus and I were all booked into one room in the same hotel.

Before we went to our room, I gathered all the leaders around me. I stood on a small stairway about three steps up and I looked at these 'pastors' in their shirts and ties and oversized suits. They were all behaving despicably, jostling for position and arguing with each other. At one point Festus slapped one of them. I knew something was very wrong, a 'holy indignation' came over me and I rebuked all of them. There were about forty men. I told them that they were not behaving like Christians let alone Pastors.

There was much skulking and shuffling of feet and, one-by-one, they began to disperse until there were only about six men left. We six went inside and I outlined my aims and objectives for the next few days. It turned out that some of the men, who had earlier disappeared into the shadows, had come with weapons (machetes and scythes) to attack me because they were told that a 'mzungu' (a white man) was coming. They associated white men with money and, as it turned out, I was the first white man that most of them had seen and I was, therefore, their golden opportunity to get rich quick. Praise God for holy boldness and divine protection!

Virtually all of my time in Omoringamu and Ogembo was fraught with deception. It was a huge learning curve. Pastor Chuma had arranged for his worship team to come over from Nairobi. They were brilliant but they had no generator for electricity, therefore, we negotiated with a local person to plug into their power supply and run a cable to the platform about half a mile away. After we had started, our power supplier insisted on more money than we originally agreed and pulled the plug on us when he didn't get it.

Vincent was my excellent translator from English to Swahili but we also needed a translator from Swahili into the Gucha language of South Kisii Lands. This translator was one of the six who remained at the hotel after our mini diaspora. I had a number of meetings with these six and prayed for them all to be baptised in the Holy Spirit. My translator went down in the Spirit and he prayed in tongues. Unfortunately, it was all an act and we were left in the lurch after he was arrested for stealing a mobile phone from a local cyber-café! Pastor Chuma, a native of South Kisii from Kiango, filled in for the missing translator.

Festus continually bad mouthed everyone around him and since we all shared a room together I was able to confront him and do something about it. After this confrontation, it transpired that Festus was lying about his position. He wasn't a pastor and he didn't have a church. He was trying to make Pastor Chuma lie for him but it all came out in the room one night and I sent Festus packing. Needless to say, he wasn't very happy about being discovered and he did his best to make life difficult for me for a while afterwards.

Eventually, he gave up trying. I have noticed that one of the most effective ways to overcome the devil is to ignore him. He is a megalomaniac and wants as much attention as possible. What do we do when a child throws a tantrum? Ignore it and eventually it stops. If we ignore the devil he will feel stupid and go away to look for someone else to pay him attention….

I had taken some top quality vitamins and supplements with me that had been gifted by a Christian pharmaceuticals company called Mannatech. We located a local nurse who was prepared to administer them for us. A few weeks after I returned to Scotland we discovered that she had started selling the vitamins and supplements and those who needed them most didn't get them. It turned out that her brother was one of those skulking pastors and he, along with the 'translator', were part of a known gang who were arrested for burglary in the village. Not only were they arrested and ended up in prison but they were run out of the town and told never to return.

This was a primitive area in many ways and it was an eye-opener for me. I learned many valuable lessons in what to do when planning a mission to a new country and culture and, more importantly, what not to do. One thing I can be thankful for is that I didn't get a headache. Apparently the local cure for a headache is to drill a hole in the sufferer's skull to let some of the pressure out. Thank God for paracetamol!

Despite all the difficulties, we finished the outreach with over one hundred new Christians making a genuine commitment to Jesus Christ. We needed to follow them up with some bona-fide Christian discipleship and that was something I would work on when I returned to Scotland. Next, on the agenda was the Nairobi Event. I flew back and Pastor Chuma met me at the airport in Nairobi. We went to his house and called a meeting there with his leaders and elders early the next morning.

At that meeting, we all agreed to meet at Pastor Chuma's home every morning to pray and to go through some basic teaching in order to set a foundation for each day. These times proved to be very fruitful becoming times of breakthrough for some of those present. While I was in Nairobi, I had determined to visit one of the largest slum districts. Pastor Chuma and I went to Kwa Njenga which was inhabited by more than one million people. This was where Pastor Chuma first lived when he came from Kiango in Kisii Lands. He worked his way out of the slums but never forgot his roots or the people who still lived there.

He had started a water business there, purchasing huge water tanks he placed them in five strategic locations. These were filled by the National Water Company during the night. He ran stand-pipes from the tanks to a variety of locations around the slum. People came with their big plastic containers and filled them up at Pastor Chuma's stand pipes paying twenty Kenyan Shillings to do so. Pastor Chuma's business prospered and he was able to buy slum property for those who had nowhere to stay. As we walked around Kwa Njenga together, Pastor Chuma was treated like a celebrity. Everyone knew him and they all called him 'Bishop'.

I wanted to visit the school that his children attended. We went together to meet Jane Wawero, the headmistress of Kwa Njenga Primary School. At that time, there were one thousand eight hundred pupils in the school with many hundreds more who wanted to attend but could not because the classrooms were already overcrowded. The pupil to teacher ratio was more than fifty to one. They desperately needed more classrooms and they also needed nourishment.

Normal practice for poor families in Kenya is for children who reach the age of eight years old or so, to be kept off school in order to go to work or to beg or to do something to bring money into the family home. The child's education is effectively stopped. These children grow up with a 'get through today by any means' mentality and by the time they are adults some of them find their way into jobs in the police force or local government, still living with the same 'scheme and scam' attitude. The result is that these agencies are full of corruption and deceit.

By feeding the children in school for free, the burden is removed from their parents to feed them. Instead of keeping the children off school the parents send them there and if the parents can get voluntarily involved in the feeding programme, all the better. In this way, a child will be physically nourished and well educated too. Within a generation, well educated and healthy young men and women will find themselves in positions of influence and they will have the potential to change the whole infrastructure of their country.

Upon returning to Scotland after my time in Africa, I was determined to do what I could to implement this vision to feed the children. I approached another Scottish charity, SIR (Scottish International Relief), and the process began to assess our proposal to help Kwa Njenga Primary School. Eventually they agreed to help and we started to feed one thousand eight hundred school children every day. More buildings, over the next few years, were added to the school compound and now the school population has doubled. Three other schools, all in Kisii Lands, have also been added to our feeding programme and at the time of writing, TheWayCM, in partnership with 'Mary's Meals' (a part of SIR), is feeding more than sixteen thousand school children every day. The work on the ground is overseen by TheWayCM's Apostolic Overseer for Kenya – Apostle Chuma, glory to God.

48

RWANDA

After my time in Kenya I flew to Rwanda, well, eventually…..
When I arrived at the airport in Nairobi, I found that my flight to
Rwanda had left early with no warning. I explained at the Kenya
Airways desk that I was on a tight schedule and I needed to get to
Rwanda. At first they weren't interested but a young man
overheard our discussion and stepped in to help. He could get me
to Kigali that day but it would mean going via Entebbe in Uganda.
This would be a long detour that would get me to Rwanda ten
hours later than planned but it was better than being twenty-four
hours late by waiting for the next scheduled direct flight to Kigali.

Rev. Emmanuel Hakizimana met me at Kigali International
Airport. I fully expected Rwanda to be heavy with sadness after the
atrocities of the 1994 genocide, but it was quite the opposite. The
Rwandese people were full of joy and showed great love.
Emmanuel took me to my very adequate hotel where I met with his
leadership team and my translator, Paul, for dinner. Paul was a
first-rate translator. He was a very short man full of vigour and
always smiling. He has translated for some of the big international
ministries, so it was an honour to have him work with me.

I outlined our aims and objectives for my mission to Rwanda. We
were having a Leaders Conference in the city and I was also going
to minister in Rev. Emmanuel's Church. We had also set aside a
day to drive across Rwanda to the western border to visit the work
in Cyangugu on the shores of Lake Kivu just this side of the border
from Bukavu in DR Congo.

I got to know the team quite well on this first mission. I could see
the needs and the potential. Emmanuel had worked in a bank and
was well educated. He had entrepreneurial skills and was

developing numerous business opportunities. He had a big vision for his work with TheWayCM in Rwanda and all around the Great Lakes. Although one of the team leaders was a school teacher, he did not believe that there were the same needs among the school children in Rwanda as there were in Kenya. The ministry went well during my time there. Driving across Rwanda gave me an opportunity to see the country. Rwanda is sometimes called, 'the land of a thousand hills' and it lives up to this description. The hills are cultivated all the way to the top and there is a sense of fertility in the land. It has the same rich red soil that was also in South Kisii Lands and bananas, tea and white maize proliferate.

In Rwanda, even more than in Kenya, the women carry everything on their heads. From the smallest child to the oldest adult, they can all be seen carrying anything from an umbrella to a whole branch of bananas – yes, that's branch not bunch! It is not unusual to see a woman carrying a huge plastic drum of water balanced impossibly on her head with a baby wrapped around her back in a blanket, standing having a conversation with another equally laden woman at the side of the road, both with great big broad African sunshine smiles that light-up their faces.

A highlight of the whole mission to Rwanda was my time ministering in Goshen Revival Church, Rev. Emmanuel's church, in Kigali. The building was made of mud with a corrugated zinc roof. There was no electricity. They had a choir of about twenty amazing voices and one 'talking drum'. The building was packed full. When the praise began, heaven came down. Everyone danced and we jumped and 'stretched our necks' like the Massai. We all overflowed from the building into the compound and soon passers-by joined us. We had a wonderful time of celebration. It was tremendous and it impacted me greatly.

49

ENLARGING THE TENT

During this missions season, I felt led to re-read and meditate on this portion of the Bible, in which Isaiah 54:2 says.... *Enlarge the place of your tent, stretch your tent curtains wide, do not hold back; lengthen your cords, strengthen your stakes.* Our 'tent curtains' were certainly 'stretched wide' and I, for one, was not 'holding back'. The 'cords', that we were lengthening, were what held 'the tent' upright. It was what made us 'upright' or right before the Lord. The 'cords' were also cords of communication, cords of accountability, cords of love, encouragement and support. 'The stakes' that were being 'strengthened' were the people and places that these cords reached.

Without the stakes to attach the cords to, the tent would fall down. These stakes are our disciples, their Home Churches and the TFL Centres. Jesus was 'staking' His reputation on them and so were The Way Christian Ministries. They must be strengthened to hold up the growing work and to maintain uprightness before God and the people around them.

Although the conferences at Kilcreggan House were our funding generator, I could not have gone on the missions, nor provided the follow-up resources, if it was not for the generosity of our faithful supporters. To them I say a huge 'thank you'. Developing the international work of TheWayCM has become my full-time ministry.

In September 2006 we began sending out our free weekly teaching called the 'Gist' in both written and video formats. We used YouTube and other Social Networking sites to reach the unsaved. I am fully persuaded that these platforms enable us to go into all the world. In fact I believe that I was doing what Jesus told His disciple Simon Peter to do when he said, *"Put out into deep water, and let down the nets for a catch."* (Luke 5:4). I hope that we will 'catch' all kinds of people using the Internet.

We also sent out the Gist through our website and by direct email to our growing database. By 2007 the written teaching was being translated into Swahili, Kinyarwanda, Nepali, Farsi and Korean. Soon to follow were Portuguese, Spanish, Telugu, Urdu, French, Kurundi and Dutch. The Foundations Course is currently available as an audio translation in Nepali, Korean, Swahili and Spanish and also as video dubbed into Urdu and Telugu. In English it is available in PAL and NTSC DVD formats.

Principally, the Gist is a Christian Discipleship resource and, as such, is made available to our Apostolic Teams and the people they oversee in various countries. Currently we are working with affiliates in up to twenty-eight countries. Many of TheWayCM members in countries where we work do not have personal access to a computer. Therefore, our overseers photocopy our weekly teaching for wider distribution. At the time of writing we estimate that, through a variety of means, the total readership of the Gist each week is about eighty thousand.

In 2007 I planned to go on three long-haul missions to new areas, plus return visits to Nepal and Israel. Firstly, I wanted to return to Nepal. Bishwa, one of Kris's brothers, had been with us for six months and was ready to go back to Nepal in February 2007. He had a good grasp of the vision for Training for Life and he had translated the Foundations Course into Nepali. Even more importantly than all that, he had been baptised in the Holy Spirit and God had given him a personal vision for the work he was to do in Nepal.

In this vision, Bishwa saw himself as a farmer sowing seeds on the mountainsides, in the isolated little village communities that are hidden away. He saw himself evangelising, leading people to salvation in Jesus and raising disciples for God's glory.

I planned a mission for April. By that time Bishwa would have had enough time, I hoped, to establish a foothold. I also wanted to have some Leaders Conferences for Pastors from all over Nepal. I took one of our trainees, Linsey, who was just about to complete one year with us. She was a TFL trainee who had also majored in photography as her TFL creative element. Tommy, my former Children's Director in Drumchapel, was also coming along and we had planned to connect with a missionary couple who were joining us for a few days. I had met one of them, Coreen, in Colorado USA the year before when I spoke at Linsey's High School graduation.

To give a little background.... In the Autumn of 2005 when a team of American youth had come on mission to Scotland. They came from Darren Patterson Christian Academy, a school in a small town high up in the Rocky Mountains of Colorado called Buena Vista. Some of the students were graduating the following year and they asked me to speak at their graduation. Linsey's family, Erik the headmaster of the school and I, all discussed the possibility of Linsey coming back with us after the graduation to be a trainee at Kilcreggan House for a year. At that time she was only seventeen years old. At the end of her year with us, she completed the mission element of her TFL course, by coming on our mission to Nepal.

During this second mission to Nepal we were able to travel much more freely because, at that time, there was a period of relative political stability in the country. We were even able to go on an elephant safari in Chitwan. While we were there we looked at some land in the town as a possible plot for a TFL Centre in Nepal. The ministry went well with a good response from the Nepalese people everywhere we went.

Pastor Krishna had planted a church in his native Gorkha in the little village where he was born called, Khoplang. It was still the early stages when we first visited, but many of the people in this village had become Christians. When he went there, Krishna was treated like a VIP. The church building has since been completed and is soon to have a new pastor. To get to Khoplang is no mean feat. At one stage we almost had to ford a river and we had to re-build a washed away road. The journey took us two days from Kathmandu.

Overnight, on the way there, we stayed in the town of Gorkha, the seat of the king in the original kingdom of Nepal. We went to visit one of the oldest original Hindu Temples where, the week before, pilgrims had made their annual pilgrimage to sacrifice offerings to their gods. Over the course of one week tens of thousands of pilgrims had offered up animal sacrifices, everything from birds to goats. When we visited, the ground was still spongy from all the spilled blood.

The WOTS books had been translated into Nepali and I am currently the co-ordinator for WOTS in Nepal. Bishwa had started some TFL groups. They were using the Nepali version of the Foundations Course and everything seemed to be in place for the next stage of our discipleship strategy.

To our horror, not long after our return to Scotland, we received the tragic news that Bishwa had been in a terrible motorcycle accident. His friend was killed and Bishwa's knee was badly injured. With no mode of transport and suffering from shock, Bishwa was unable to pursue his vision and, sadly, his position as TFL Co-ordinator for Nepal was never fully realised. Not long after this, Bishwa left Nepal to study in London. Within weeks of our return from Nepal, Linsey returned to the States. She continued, from a distance, to help me with some IT admin work until she enrolled in a university course studying Photography and Journalism at which she has excelled.

Another TFL trainee at Kilcreggan House was Anna. She enrolled soon after I baptised her in the Jordan on one of our trips to Israel. She was with us for about six months before Linsey came. Anna fell in love with my IT helper Andrew. She left at Christmastime 2007 before the Nepal mission. Originally, I was to solemnise their wedding but it clashed with our Nepal mission dates. Both Anna and Andrew were a tremendous help in our ministry and although we were very happy for them to be so in love and married, we lost their valuable input. Andrew has continued to help me but a lot less frequently. We remain good friends today.

During 2006 we started to receive a flow of volunteers from South Korea. Euisang was the first of them. After six months, as Euisang moved on, Anna Lee joined us. These first volunteers from Korea were a great blessing to us and we remember them with great fondness. While with us Anna Lee translated the Foundations Course into Korean.

The second of these long-haul missions took me back to Mexico. Nancy and I had gone to Mexico in 2004 with an American friend, Jack, who pastored in Glasgow. We went as part of a group of six, first to Los Angeles where Jack had family. We stayed in Hollywood Hills with Jack's sister, who was an estate agent. From there we hired a car and drove south down the coastline of California to Mexico and into Mexicali where we ministered for a few days. I had a great time with the Mexicans. I still love all things Spanish. It was wonderful to be able to prattle away with them in their own language.

On this mission, I was going, on my own to Villahermosa in the Tabasco region of Mexico on the Yucatan Peninsula in the Bay of Mexico. Apostle Esteban Montalvo Copto, whom I met at Wayne

Cordeiro's Practicum in Hawaii in 2002, was to be my host. After many delays on a journey totalling more than twenty-four hours, I eventually arrived at Villahermosa Airport, via Mexico City. Esteban's big happy smile soon smoothed off my frayed edges. I had an amazing time with Esteban, his wife Norma and his family.

I ministered throughout the region, both with and without a translator, in a few of Esteban's churches. However, it wasn't all ministry. We also visited Esteban's friends and family and we did some sight-seeing. One day he took me to a place called 'Paraiso' ('Paradise' in English) which was amazingly beautiful. It was our day off from ministry and we swung in hammocks in the warm balmy breeze just above the golden sands under the gently swaying coconut palms; aaahhh.... life at the sharp end of Christian ministry! When the food was ready, we were roused to eat a feast of smoked oysters washed down with coconut milk from coconuts freshly cut from said swaying palm trees....

We had a conference with all the gathered leaders from Apostle Esteban's churches in that part of Mexico. It was an opportunity for me to share about TFL and the Foundations Course that was now translated into Spanish. The anointing was strong and many people were impacted by the power of the Holy Spirit during the ministry time afterwards. Esteban's work has continued to expand and our friendship has developed. There is no doubt that we will work together throughout South America.

50

THE PHILIPPINES

In September 2007, Nancy and I went together on the third of my sheduled long-haul missions. This time we went to the Cebu City, on the island of Cebu, in the Philippines. The contacts for this mission had come through our friend Ian. Ian was Scottish, in fact he was born and raised in Kilcreggan. However, as a teenager he had joined the RAF (Royal Air Force) to learn about photography. After finishing his time in the RAF he stayed on in south-east Asia working as a freelance filmmaker. He moved to Hawaii and found work with CNN and some travel channels. He travelled extensively around the word making a living as a film maker. For the past few years he has been based in Cebu.

Ian came across TheWayCM on the internet. He was looking for connections back to his birth place Kilcreggan and he first got in touch with me in 2005. He came to stay with us and while he was with us he did some filming for me. His trip coincided with me teaching a group from our Prophetic Bible Teachers Course. Ian filmed the teaching. When I saw what Ian did it prompted me to look at ways of sending out a complimentary Gist video to accompany my written teaching. This started a huge learning curve that was to lead to my learning how to film and edit digital videos. I did this firstly for the social networking sites like YouTube (see PeterStanway YouTube), and eventually it led to making good enough quality short videos that are regularly shown on the Christian satellite network UCB (United Christian Broadcasters).

Ian came back and stayed at Kilcregan House a few of times. He was keen to get me over to Cebu to minister. However, although he was open to the Lord, Ian was not yet born again and therefore had virtually no contact with Christians. An opportunity came about in a most unexpected way. One day, in a small restaurant, Ian overheard an American talking about his teaching job at a Bible School in Cebu. Ian waited until he had a chance and then started up a conversation with Greg, a Reach Global missionary who had been in Cebu City with Hannah, his wife and their daughter Suni, for around one year.

Ian told him about me and one thing led to another. Greg had connections with many of the AOG Pastors in the city. Ian put us in touch with each other and a tour was set up for me to minister in a number of Pentecostal Churches and the AOG Bible College in Cebu City. All of this was quite ironic as Greg himself was an evangelical and not at all Pentecostal with little or no personal experience of the 'charismata' or gifts of the Holy Spirit.

Ian, with his camera rolling, met Nancy and I at Mactan-Cebu International Airport and we all went back to Greg's missionary home for a meeting and to talk through the aims and objectives of our mission to Cebu. Greg's home was very comfortable and it was to be our home for the duration of our mission, that is, with the exception of the next night. Ian, who had done some filming work on a large resort at the north of Cebu Island had called-in a favour and arranged for Nancy and I to spend a night there.

Therefore, the day after we arrived in Cebu, a private taxi collected us from the entrance to one of the largest hotels in the city. We were chauffeured for two hours along the east coast, through the pleasant farming and fishing area of Sogod. Just after Sogod is the fashionable Alegre Beach Resort. This was to be our home for the next twenty-four hours. Alegre is a lovely spot, a true getaway, lusciously verdant with walks through coconut groves, beautiful clusters of hanging flowers and a breath-taking private bay. The white sandy beach perfectly sets off the inviting blue of the water. The private villas have thatched roofs. The huge pamper bathrooms are, apparently, a favourite with honeymooners.

It was perfect and just what Nancy and I needed. We felt extremely spoiled and during our time there we were able to catch-up with ourselves and adjust after all the time zones we had passed through. We had changed aeroplanes in Amsterdam and Manila. The actual flying time was eighteen hours, not including the short hops. The next day we were chauffeured back to Cebu City and straight into ministry. Our time in the Philippines was excellent. The ministry was powerful and well received. We visited lots of restaurants and experienced first-hand the extremes of poverty and wealth that co-exist there.

One of our highlights was meeting Greg and Hannah's daughter, Suni. She was a child prodigy. At the age of three she was reading four books every day; advanced learning books not unlike encyclopaedias. Hannah is Chinese so Suni spoke Chinese as well as English and she was learning German along with her dad. Greg was planning to come to Aberdeen, Scotland to study for a PhD and the books he was required to study were only available in German. She felt easy around a computer and she played the piano competently, with two hands.

On the night before we were due to leave the Philippines, Nancy suddenly became quite seriously ill with sickness and dizziness. She would not allow me to contact a doctor or take her to hospital because she didn't want our return to the UK to be delayed. Suni asked if she could pray for 'Mrs Stanway' and we all readily agreed. She knelt at the side of Nancy's bed, took hold of her hand and prayed, 'God, heal Mrs Stanway'. That was enough. Within minutes Nancy started to feel better and before I was due to go out to minister at the last meeting, Nancy was up and about and starting to pack. Her sickness never came back.

51

ICON

In November 2007 Nancy and I returned to Israel. This time we went on a leaders training tour in order for us to be able to take people on tour to the Holy Land. It was different from the two previous tours but as awesome as ever. We have now been trained and we cannot wait to take our own tour to Israel.

It had been quite a year for travelling and our ground-breaking missions needed a lot of follow-up to consolidate what had happened and to ensure that TFL was up-and-running throughout the network of Home Churches that were spreading like wild fire across the nations.

Throughout 2007, Nancy and I had been discussing the best way forward for the work at Kilcreggan House. We were busy and the work was extremely demanding. We began to formulate a three-phase development plan that would unfold over the next five years. It would be a multi-million pounds (GBPs) major redevelopment of the three-and-a-half acres of land and out-buildings around the main mansion. Our idea was, in phase one, to build permanent dwellings that we would offer for sale to Christians and in doing so we would develop an eco-friendly modern Christian community with state-of-the-art facilities including, in phase two, a fitness suite with pool and a multi-purpose community centre. Phase three was to develop the back land wooded area with some large log cabins in one area and in the other area an apartment block built in the same style as Kilcreggan House mansion with a turret, and so on. The house itself would become ultra high-spec accommodation for up to twenty guests with their own en-suite pamper facilities and sumptuous luxuries; a place of blessing for ministers in active service for Jesus.

We needed to put a planning team together and, one person at a time, we did this. Auchlochan Retirement Village, near Lesmahagow is a place that had impressed us for many years. The standard of excellence at every level was second to none. It had won European awards for its many qualities. Robert was the main builder for the seven hundred and fifty dwellings that Auchlochan had grown to become. It had its own lake and hotel as well as offering accommodation at every level from small flats to grand detached homes.

Robert's wife Shona had been a guest at Kilcreggan House. I asked her if she thought that Robert would be open to offer us advice and she suggested that we went to speak with him on-site at Auchlochan. I made an appointment and Nancy and I went down with a little PowerPoint presentation I had prepared that outlined our vision. I showed it to Robert and before we could say 'please' he said to us, 'So, do you want me to build this for you?' We were gob-smacked, we couldn't have asked for more. We had our builder.

Next we needed an architect. We found out the name of the firm that designed the interiors of church buildings that we liked, the King's in Motherwell among them, and it turned out to be a firm of architects that had also worked for Robert. He set up an appointment for the four of us at Kilcreggan House. I was busy on the phone when Daniel, their representative, arrived. Nancy met him first and introduced herself. It turned out that they knew each other from when they were young children and had attended the same church in Kilmarnock.

I entered the room and immediately I thought that I recognised Daniel. Nancy said, 'no, it's me who knows Daniel'. Undeterred, I pressed my point and, sure enough, when Daniel's family left Kilmarnock they moved to a place near Fernhill where I was living and we attended the same primary school for a few years. Not only that but Daniel later attended the Glasgow School of Art to study Architecture around the same time as I was there studying Mixed Media in another part of the campus. It certainly seemed as though God was in this.

Daniel drafted some outline plans and we presented them to the local Planning Department. They came out to see us and gave verbal consent to continue. Everything was moving along nicely, although a little seed of doubt began to germinate inside my spirit. This little nagging doubt coincided with our third trip to the Holy Land. By the end of this trip we were very familiar with all the historical buildings, their dynasty and their architects. Our guide spoke so endearingly of each building that he made it into a religious icon and that, in turn, sounded an alarm in my spirit.....

52

"WHAT HAVE I CALLED YOU TO DO?"

Wherever we went in the world, Nancy and I would invariably meet someone who knew of or had a connection to Kilcreggan House. The house was built in 1880 by the owner of the Donaldson Shipping Line for his Christian son and it has, almost always, been occupied by Christian groups or individuals since that time. It has been featured in books written about previous owners and their guests, among them Austin Sparks and his friend Watchman Nee. The people who owned the house before us were WEC (World Evangelisation for Christ) founded by C.T. Studd. They are the largest missionary organisation in the UK responsible for sending thousands of people out as missionaries all over the world. In some ways, Kilcreggan House had become iconic and I questioned whether we were now in danger of 'worshipping' this icon. The very idea of that was absurd but, insidiously and unconsciously, it may just be possible that we were.

Christmas 2007 was fast approaching and it was time to do the Christmas shopping for our children, grandchildren and friends. It was a good time but not without its stress. I was looking forward to having our family gathered together around us for the festivities. Suddenly, on Christmas Eve during the day, out of the blue from nowhere, I was crippled with pains across my chest. Nancy bundled me into our car and rushed me to see the doctor. He suspected that I was having a heart attack.
'No, I can't be. I've got a strong heart!' I exclaimed
He told Nancy to take me straight over to our local hospital, The Vale of Leven, about forty-five minutes drive away. I was so convinced was that nothing was seriously wrong that I told Nancy to go via the house in order for me to pick up some work to do while I was waiting to be seen at the hospital. I climbed up three flights of stairs to my study to fetch what I wanted. After

examination at A&E it was confirmed that I had, indeed, had a heart attack and I was put to bed in a ward and hooked up to monitors. I spent the next few days there.

2008 started with me on doctor's orders to rest from work and I was put on a vigorous regime of cardio-vascular exercises. When I wasn't exercising, Nancy and I had quality time to pray and talk together. One of the things that we discussed was this 'niggle' that I felt inside. Nancy wasn't convinced, after all Kilcreggan House was our 'nest' and Nancy had been preparing it for us to spend the rest of our lives there. The bulldozers were ready to start phase one in early Spring. Surely I was wrong, she thought.

One day, loud and clear, I felt the Lord ask me a question, 'What have I called you to do? Is it property development or is it people development?' That was enough for me. As far as I was concerned, the building project was scuppered. Not only that but I believe that the Lord was telling me to stop what we were doing at Kilcreggan House and to sell it; to 'streamline for efficiency' by downsizing. Well, Nancy was not a happy bunny! she wasn't ready to hear all that. She needed to hear from God for herself. She began to earnestly seek God and over the next few weeks she heard Him speak to her personally and we made plans to put Kilcreggan House on the market.

Firstly, we had to have the house valued and two independent Estate Agents put a market value on the house at over one million pounds. We prepared a beautiful schedule in a brochure format, took out advertisements in the main property newspapers and earnestly began to sell the house. We contacted all of our Christian friends and ministry associates, soon people began to respond. Many people came to see the house, many promises were made. There were lots of highs and lows. It was like riding on an emotional rollercoaster and then, seemingly out of the blue, the government announced that the country was in a recession. Banks collapsed, huge companies went bust, high street shops started to close. The whole world was in financial meltdown and nobody was buying houses.

'Surely, God is bigger than a recession', we said. 'All the greater glory to Him when He sells Kilcreggan House, amen?' Ten years after we started repaying the loan, Kilcreggan House was bought and paid for. Although we were no longer facilitating conferences or even accepting guests to stay at Kilcreggan House, month by month we were amazed at how the money came in from all kinds of sources to pay the ongoing overheads and bills.

A bonus of my stay-at-home year, 2008, was that Nancy and I had time to enjoy quality time with each other and with our family and friends; a time to develop relationships. We were able to visit our parents in their latter years and, in hindsight, that was a special gift from God.

Israel qualified as a car mechanic and left college in the summer of 2008. He began to look for practical work in preparation for his call to live and work in the land of Israel, the Holy Land. I was at home and so was my son, thank you Lord. Another area of great blessings was in the time that I was able to spend with my step-daughters; Pamela and Dawn and our grandchildren; Daniel, Rachel, Stephanie, Naomi and Bethany. I was able to attend their birthday parties and just be their 'Papa'. I loved that. Our sixth grandchild, Sam, was born in October 2008.

The one word that God had given from the time Kilcreggan House first went on the market was that the sale would happen, 'suddenly'. When He first spoke this word to me, in my spirit, I knew the context was as it was in the Upper Room in Jerusalem when the disciples were waiting on the promise of the Holy Spirit. They had to wait until the tenth day before the promise from Jesus was fulfilled..... *'Suddenly a sound like the blowing of a violent wind came from heaven and filled the whole house where they were sitting.'* (Acts 2:2). I am sure that those ten days must have seemed like a lifetime to the one hundred and twenty people who were gathered there, but it took that passage of time to bring them all together, in agreement, in body, soul and spirit. The 'suddenly' came when there was absolute unity, a perfect harmony, among the group and unconditional, undoubting faith in what Jesus had said.

I believe that the dawn is breaking on our 'tenth day' and our 'suddenly' sale is imminent. I am already planning to start my next book, the sequel to this one, with the sale of Kilcreggan House!

53

PIONEERS AND SETTLERS

Rather than 'mark time' waiting for the house to sell, I realised that I needed to continue with the on-going work of the ministry. That is precisely what I did and the work has continued to grow. As 2008 progressed I began to make plans to go on mission.

In 2009 I was able to visit Pakistan, Nepal, Darjeeling, Kenya, Rwanda and Uganda. What a privilege it is to go to all those countries. Our missions are not just a fleeting visit. They are an attempt to get to know the culture and customs of the indigenous people. I aim to build-up and strengthen our relationships. I want to connect with them and make every effort to understand them. I try to integrate into their families when I am with them, to share their food, their language and their customs. Nancy says I become like a different person when I go on mission, but surely that's how it should be. I will never be African or Asian but when I am in their countries I want to do all I can to bond with them. My ministry is about so much more than simply making disciples out of Christians. I go on mission to develop relationships that develop into friendships.

When teaching our TFL trainees about missions, I discovered an important insight. In a broad sweep, people divide into two general categories; pioneers or settlers. I am a pioneer.

Pioneers are trailblazers. Metaphorically, they love to cut their way through the jungle, removing whatever obstacle comes into their path. Settlers, on the other hand, come along behind the pioneers and they collect, they gather up, what the pioneers leave behind and they turn the felled trees into houses and the cleared land into farms.

Both types of people are essential and, in fact, they need each other. However, settlers are freaked-out by pioneers and the idea of being one scares them. Nancy is a settler. She is a home-builder and she is excellent at it. It is vital when working with a missions team that we do not confuse which category each person belongs to and, once identified, do all that we can to encourage and strengthen them in their calling.

54

ENDINGS AND BEGINNINGS

On May 7th, 2010 Nancy's dad, 'Papa Stewart', passed away after a long, hard battle with Alzheimer's. He was eighty-nine years old. We could trace the beginning of Papa's Alzheimer's to the death of his beloved wife Jean who had died in 2001. Papa had stayed with us at Kilcreggan House for five years. Firstly, on a part time basis then, latterly, full time. During that time, Papa loved to help around the house and at over eighty years of age he would vacuum, help with bed making, wash dishes and scrub pots until you could see your face in them. He thoroughly enjoyed his time at Kilcreggan House and it gave his life a purpose. He felt able to contribute to our ministry. Sadly, the time came when he needed specialist care and he spent the last years of his life in a very caring nursing home that specialised in looking after people with Alzheimers and similar illnesses.

At the end of May 2010, Nancy and I embarked on a five weeks ministry tour, coast-to-coast, through six states in the USA. We were only twelve days into it when a five a.m. phone call from home woke me up. It was my extremely distraught sister telling me that my mother had died. We had to spring into action in order for me to get home to conduct the funeral service. We were home in less than twenty-four hours and my mother's funeral was on the third day after we got back. She had died exactly one month to the day after Papa. Over the years our relationship with my mum and Papa grew deeper and stronger. We were able to spend valued, precious times with them and we thank God that we did.

Although we had to cut our American tour short, much was accomplished in the time that we were there. We met amazing people and saw some fantastic places. One of the people that we met was David Yanez. He and his family were our hosts in

Houston, Texas. I had been broadcasting a weekly radio show on David's Network, RevMediaNetwork.com, for about six months. David is also a book publisher and it is his company that published this very book that you are reading.

Throughout 2010 I made every effort to consolidate the work in the countries around the world that I have previously visited on mission and I began to make plans to go on mission to an increasing number of new countries. I built new websites, tidied-up old ones and found new ways to reach our own people and new people using a wide range of technical developments and Social Networking platforms.

55

IN CONCLUSION

My life has been so blessed. It has been an amazing journey so far and full of God's grace. His love has rescued me from a life of destruction and despair. He has raised me up to be a follower of Jesus Christ and He is using me in ways I could never have imagined. God is faithful and true. I am excited and I look forward to discovering what adventures He has in store for me in the future.

As an artist, I discovered that one of the most difficult things about painting is to know when to stop. It is so easy to go beyond that point and ruin the painting. I feel I have just about said enough in this book. I have both laughed and cried as I remembered the details of what I have recounted here. It has been, at times, pleasurable and painful. I believe that I am on a perpetual learning curve and I wouldn't want it any other way. The Bible says that we only know in part that which will be revealed more fully when we see Jesus face to face. Of one thing I am certain, and that is, that this wee boy from Glasgow is delighted that he discovered how to cry.

When I first cried in a healthy way, it was through brokenness and remorse that led to repentance. My tears opened a door that allowed God's mercy and compassion to come flooding into my heart. It happened in Mijas, Spain at the age of thirty-three and it was liberating. It changed my life. My back-to-the-wall survival tactics could not stop God's love from overwhelming me and I found the missing piece of my salvation jigsaw. I was baptised in the Holy Spirit. Even although I had wandered far away from the Lord, He had not left me. It is only because of His grace that I am still here to tell my tale. Every day I thank God for the breath I breathe, I do not take it for granted.

It is my hope that people from all walks of life and backgrounds will read this book. Thank you for reading it. Maybe you're a Christian or maybe you're not. Maybe you were and you have drifted away from Jesus. The good news is that Jesus Christ came to the earth, was crucified and died, was buried and rose again for you, that's right, you.

I once saw a crazy looking tattooed, wild-haired youth wearing a t-shirt that said, *'Body Piercing Saved My Life'*. My eyes followed him as he strolled past me and, there on the back of the t-shirt, was a full body print of Jesus on the cross. Jesus was nailed to the cross. He was pierced for our sins. Without Jesus in my life, I would most certainly be dead; nothing surer. Jesus Christ has saved my life many times but He has done much more than that. He has baptised me with the Holy Spirit and He has given me eternal life. He enables me to live my life to the full as a victorious born again Christian believer.

Jesus Christ is standing at the door of your heart today and He's knocking. The handle of the door is on your side, will you open it and allow him to come in? Can you say, 'Come into my heart Lord Jesus. Be my Saviour and my Lord, from this day forward and forever. Come Holy Spirit and fill me with power. Help me to follow Jesus every day. Amen'.

Now, let your adventure begin.

COMMENTS

"No one can actually say they've 'worked' with Peter on any project ... Peter's inner strength and charisma subsumes the project adding a whole new dimension to everyone concerned. Primarily, he's not like your average clergyman, he actually does 'what it says on the tin' in that he gets down with the drug abused, homeless and broken and somehow finds the strength to both say AND 'do' the right things for them! On a damp, dismal January morning, when the cold was so fierce that the mere thought of travelling seemed foolish at best, I've personally seen him spending himself delivering both hot food and loving care to the desperate and needy on the mean streets of Glasgow ... and yet, and how incongruous is this, he somehow also found the time to get hold of something that most of us would consider rather opulent given the circumstances - carpets for a young family just starting life together! Jesus with skin on, in a world that's forgotten ..."

November 13, 2009

Warren Wysocki, *Managing Director , EurekaStep Ltd*

"Peter is a person who is clearly inspired and driven by a calling to his ministry by our Lord. Peter's determination and drive to his ministry is obviously led by the Spirit and is evidenced by the people's lives who he has touched both here and across numerous countries. Peter's witness has crossed many cultures."

April 6, 2010

Rick Grainger, *Owner , Trunky Inc*

"Rev. Peter Stanway is a true man of God. He has a powerful anointing, and is always seeking Gods Best. He has great compassion for the lost, and seeks to impact the world with Gods Word and Gods Spirit, even when the cost for him personally is high. His knowledge of the Word is vast, but he is not interested in tickling people's ears: he seeks to catapult them into Gods plan. It was a great privilege for me to serve this Man of God. That was an awesome time, where I continuously experienced Gods hand and blessing. Even though it was 10 years ago, my continued contact with him is a constant source of blessing for me and my family. And the principles I learnt from him are still a source of guidance for me."

November 24, 2009

Evert van de Waal, *Assistant to the Minister , The Way Christian Ministries*

"Peter and his wife Nancy were invaluable to me when I was seeking answers to my own personal spiritual quest. Peter gave me direction that was respectful of me as a person, allowing me to grow and take responsibility for my own learning and growth. I spent some happy times with Peter and Nancy and learned so much from them, their open heartedness, their welcome and their loving hospitality. They are both great teachers in a very unobtrusive and gentle way but their lessons still challenge and help one to grow. If anyone is looking for help in spiritual growth, either online or in person, I would have no hesitation in recommending my mentors and friends Peter and Nancy Stanway."

November 12, 2009
John McMahon

"Peter Stanway is one of the most hard working men I have ever met. This has been born out of his passionate desire to introduce people to Jesus Christ - and to help them grow in their faith in Him - and consequently he works tirelessly towards that goal. He and his wife Nancy make an incredible team."

November 12, 2009
Bill Partington, Head of Ministry, United Christian Broadcasters

"Peter has pushed me out of my theological comfort zone...I did not like that...he has frightened me with some of his stories....didn't like that either....to the lady who sat beside me on the plane and may have heard me sniff after reading about the liver transplant....it's ok.....boys from NZ do cry."

Gary Hoogvliet, Director of Broadcasting, United Christian Broadcasters Ltd

The Way Christian Ministries

Peter Stanway

The Way Christian Ministries

Kilcreggan House

Kilcreggan

G84 0JT

Scotland UK

E: peter@thewaycm.com

O: +44 (0)1436 842318

M: +44 (0)7764 895309

W: www.peterstanwaybooks.com

Charity No. : SCO27189

*Directions to Glenelg

The road to Glenelg, if you ever want to visit, starts at the head of Loch Duich, at Shiel Bridge, where a minor road branches off, the A87 towards Kyle of Lochalsh. It makes its way across the Mam Ratagan Pass at a height of eleven-hundred feet before dropping down the side of Glen More into Glenelg at the water's edge on Kyle Rhea near the Sound of Sleat.

Lightning Source UK Ltd.
Milton Keynes UK
UKOW031826080212

186920UK00001B/14/P